FALL
IN LOVE
··
FOR
··

Life

FALL IN LOVE

FOR

Life

INSPIRATION FROM A 73-YEAR MARRIAGE

by

BARBARA "CUTIE" COOPER

with

KIM COOPER AND CHINTA COOPER

CHRONICLE BOOKS

SAN FRANCISCO

Library of Congress Cataloging-in-Publication Data
available.

ISBN 978-1-4521-0916-9

Manufactured in China

Designed by TRACY SUNRIZE JOHNSON

10 9 8 7 6 5 4 3 2

Chronicle Books LLC
680 Second Street
San Francisco, California 94107
www.chroniclebooks.com

FOR
HARRY

When my wife started giving free advice to the whole world, I warned them: listen to Barbara and she'll either put you in the White House or the poorhouse. But the truth is, Barbara is a pretty sharp girl. I've benefited from her advice since 1937, and usually, she steers me right.

Ask her; I don't do anything without Barbara's advice. Her secret is that she plays things in moderation, thinks about it when she answers you, and she observes everything. There's a great deal of wisdom inside every suggestion, if you take time to look at it.

—HARRY COOPER, 2010

✳ CONTENTS ✳

CHAPTER 4: HARDSHIPS AND CHALLENGES

CHAPTER 5: GROWING OLD TOGETHER
. . . AND GOING ON ALONE

INTRODUCTION

IF YOU WERE TO HAVE ASKED THEM IN 2008, when their blog began picking up steam, our grandparents Barbara and Harry Cooper (a.k.a. Cutie and Pop Pop) would say that they don't understand what the fuss is all about. They'd tell you they're just your basic boy-meets-girl story, and they haven't explored uncharted lands or cured a disease. But, to us, they have always been the wisest people we know. Their marriage of seventy-three years inspires awe. Everyone who met them or sees their video blogs wants to know the same thing: How have you kept your love alive for so many years? This little book reveals the secrets behind their seven-decades-long love story, the challenges and triumphs they've faced together, and the strengths they've drawn upon to stay bonded, together, for life.

On the auspicious fall day when Cutie and Pop Pop exchanged their wedding vows, FDR was president, a can of soup cost a nickel, and the rent on a four-room Hollywood apartment was a lavish fifty dollars. They celebrated their tenth anniversary the year of the Black Dahlia and Bugsy Siegel killings, their twenty-fifth on the eve of the Cuban Missile Crisis, and their fiftieth during the Iran-Contra Affair. And they celebrated year seventy-two by regularly tweeting and posting to their Facebook fan page—with a little help from us grandchildren.

Though we are half sisters, and separated in age by more than twenty years, we've always shared the understanding that our grandparents were incredible characters and the two people in our family we most wanted to be around. But it wasn't until we started shooting video blogs with them in 2008 that we discovered that their appeal extended well beyond our blood-line. Our grandparents had recently moved back to Los Angeles after three decades in suburbia, and at ninety-one and ninety-six, they were adapting to the new patterns of an assisted-living facility, just as we were adapting to our new roles as their primary caregivers following the sudden deaths of both of their children, our aunt Carol and our father, Jan.

We started The OGs blog (that's The Original Grandparents blog, to the uninitiated) as a lark, something fun we could do together in their apartment. The playful videos we shot and uploaded to YouTube weren't really meant for anyone to see, but they soon attracted a cult following of enthusiasts who responded to our grandparents' wry observations and affection for one another. A songwriter friend, Thessaly Lerner, volunteered to write them a jingle, and once we'd heard the biographical earworm of "Oh wow, oh gee, it's the OGs," the whole enterprise felt somehow professional, like a real TV show. If the world wanted Cutie and Pop Pop, we'd just have to give them to the world.

And so we made and shared our miniature movies of Cutie doling out advice to her fans and Pop Pop musing on the possibilities of time travel, costume parties, and family outings. Each time we showed up with the camera, they'd act put-upon and remind us that nobody could possibly care about a couple of little old people who loved each other—but we could see by the way they lit up when the red light came on that they couldn't get enough of the attention, and they loved to make us laugh. The thing is, their advice really resonated. Even though they found themselves in a very different world than the one in which they fell in love, their simple yet profound perspectives on what really matters in life were just what modern people needed to hear. So much so that the *Los Angeles Times* featured Cutie and Pop Pop on the front page. What a thrill to see our family celebrated in that way. The *TODAY* show, CNN, and *All Things Considered* all followed, each reporting on the story with its own spin. The OGs were seen on Thai, Austrian, and Japanese TV, and we discovered that their message of a lifetime of love struck a chord in translation, too. It shouldn't be a surprise. People are pretty much the same everywhere, and you don't have to speak English to feel a pang of envy when you see an old couple as madly in love as our grandparents. That's a connection that's sought every day, by people in every part of the world.

As soon as we took over the caregiving duties for our grandparents, we talked about what we would do if one of them sickened or died before the other. Pop Pop was five years older, but Cutie was frail after a heart attack, so there wasn't a sense that one of them was likely to fade first. We decided that we wanted to give them a living situation in which they could enjoy all the happiness and togetherness that was possible while ensuring that they both had a full life to turn to if one of them couldn't keep up. So we found a retirement home where they could both stay on, even if one of them needed more medical care than the other. We were so gratified to see them both thriving in a new situation, which they'd been ambivalent about, and delighted that they got to enjoy a couple of good years together. When Pop Pop got sick and moved into the nursing ward of their retirement home, we encouraged Cutie to look after herself, stay active, and express her feelings of fear and frustration, feelings that we shared with her. Our grandparents' love was such a powerful thing that it touched everyone around them. Our whole family drew from this well of love as we went through the difficult process of letting Pop Pop go. He died peacefully in October 2010.

We told Cutie that we really hoped she'd stick around for a while, and after thinking it over, she decided to our great relief that she wasn't ready to follow her husband into the unknown.

We threw ourselves back into working on the blog. Word got out about our grandmother's free therapeutic services, and soon Cutie's e-mail account was flooded with desperate cries for help from young people with problems that needed the healing touch of a wise old grandmother. Ask Grandma Anything is the name of her blog, and ask they did—about fixing their marriages, curing phobias, mending friendships gone awry, and embarking on career paths not taken. Cutie was initially flabbergasted, but then dug in with gusto, filming video answers to some questions and shooting off strongly worded e-mails to those who just couldn't wait. "Dear Abby has had her day," she announced. "Now it's *my* turn!"

This book tackles the challenges facing anyone who wants to form a successful romantic partnership, get along with his or her parents, raise some nice children, enjoy his or her career, and have a fulfilling life.

Through the lessons of our grandparents' inspiring romance, we'll share real-world examples of how to get on the right path as a young person and stay there well into your old age. We think Cutie and Pop Pop are pretty sharp cookies, and since most people aren't lucky enough to have such wise old folks in their families, their wisdom ought to be shared.

When we were growing up, in the late twentieth century, it was a novelty to encounter a family comprised of a mother and father, both on their first marriage, raising their own children. Divorce, stepsiblings, single parenting, dads or moms out of the picture—family dynamics that were uncommon and somewhat scandalous in our grandparents' younger days were sitcom fodder to us. But even as our own parents fought—and in Kim's case, divorced—we looked to Cutie and Pop Pop's loving marriage with undisguised awe.

And although they were quick to admit their marriage wasn't perfect (and sometimes it wasn't even fun), divorce or separation was simply not a serious consideration—they were in it together for the long haul.

It was the two of them against the world, from 1937 until we lost Pop Pop, in fall 2010. We feel so honored to have been able to experience our grandparents' connection, and to share the story of their love affair, through their blog and this book. In a throwaway world, how amazing it is to find something so delicate yet so abiding.

In the end, we've learned there's no magic formula for making a marriage work or making a life fulfilling. But we think Cutie's story has a lot to offer anyone looking for guidance while navigating his or her own relationships and discovering the life he or she wants to be living. Cutie agrees. "I'll tell you some of our secrets for finding love and happiness, but your secret is something you'll have to figure out for yourself. If our story helps you get there, I'm happy to share."

—KIM COOPER AND CHINTA COOPER, LOS ANGELES

FALLING ɪɴ LOVE ....

ZING WENT THE STRINGS

When I met Harry, in 1937, I was a very sophisticated twenty-year-old girl who thought I knew it all and really knew nothing. He was twenty-five and much more worldly, but gentleman enough not to let it show. We "met cute," as they say in Hollywood, on my mother's couch, where my friend Lillian had parked him while I spruced up for our three-person tennis date. Harry was Lil's big brother, and she was a doll, so he came with fine references.

I wasn't officially in the market for a boyfriend, because I was in a long-distance relationship with a guy I'd met in New York the year before. But the New Yorker hadn't been as attentive as he should have been, and I couldn't help but notice how cute Harry was, with his thick, curly hair; wide brown eyes; and great big smile.

Harry couldn't help but notice how cute I was, either, since my idea of tennis attire included high-heeled shoes. Of course, I knew this wasn't traditional footwear for the sport, but I wasn't much of a player anyway, and how else was the world supposed to know I had gorgeous legs? So off we went to the tennis courts, where we hit a few balls back and forth, and it became clear that Harry liked me. Lucky me. Or lucky him. Lucky both of us. He came back to my mother's house, and she fed us.

That was our first date, but I can't really tell you much about our second or third dates, since he never really left! We didn't know about dates, anyway. You call it a date; you call it a day; you call it a night. We just wanted to be together, and we were. When Harry wasn't at work—when we met, he was

driving a truck and doing some selling for a wholesale purveyor of gourmet Swedish foods—he was hanging around my mother's house, and so
was I, which meant we were together. It was a very homespun thing. He
didn't knock on our door with flowers in his hand. He just came with his
great big smile, and that was enough for me.

Harry was a very considerate young man, a nice Jewish boy. Not a big
mouth, and not a show-off. To my surprise, not only did my very picky
Old World papa not run him off, but he welcomed him. My mother liked
him, too, and my aunt absolutely adored him. I have to admit the older
folks knew a thing or two about character, and they recognized the potential in Harry even before I saw it.

And so we were a couple. The nice thing was that we didn't need a
lot of money to enjoy ourselves—which was good, because we didn't have
any. The Depression was on, and everyone was used to making do. Let me
tell you about our big nights out. He'd pick me up, and we'd drive around
in his car, hold hands, and talk about how lucky we were to have found
each other, then go to a hamburger joint and have an inexpensive meal,
over which we'd linger as though it were a three-course banquet. Then
he'd take me home. Always the gentleman.

If we had money to put gas in the car, we would do that, and then drive
to the mountains or the beach. You're lucky when you live in California,
where the million-dollar views are free. If we had some food, we took it
to a park and made it a picnic. Sometimes we'd walk along the sidewalk,
window-shopping in the fancy stores. All these years later, I have such a
vivid memory of us coming out of the movies in Pasadena, arm in arm,
looking in the window of a jewelry store, and Harry pointing out the dia-
mond ring he wished he could buy for me. That's when I knew he wanted
me to be his wife, and that ring has always been mine in my heart, although
our actual commitment to one another didn't cost us anything at all.

And, of course, on our dates we would talk and talk and talk. Once
we got serious, we wanted to learn as much as there was to know about
each other, because you don't want to marry a stranger. And I knew it was

right, because I discovered that I had no interest in being with another man or boy—I wanted to be with Harry all the time.

It seemed like he didn't give me time to think about other things. When we met, my life was very simple. I was out of school, living with my parents, and I only had a few close friends. Suddenly, Harry was there, and my life was exciting and full.

And Harry had room for me in his life. He worked hard, played tennis, and went out with the boys, but when I came along, he made a Barbara-size space in the very center of his world, and made sure I knew it.

I'd had some boyfriends in the past. They were tall, they were small, they were other things, but I had always found fault with each of them. Harry was the first person who I found no fault with at all. And later, if something about him bothered me, I let it go, because when you love somebody, you learn to love his mistakes, too.

These other guys, they thought they were big shots, with big mouths, know-it-all types. When a date ended, I was in no hurry to have another one. Harry was different. He was quiet and gentle. He didn't try to impress me, which was refreshing. There were no surprises with him. Harry was an open book, very sincere, very honest.

He thought that I was smart and beautiful, and he told me so, which felt wonderful. He said he wanted to give me the world, which was something all my other boyfriends said—but when Harry said it, I believed him. And the truth was, I didn't need the world; I just needed his time and his love, which he gave to me gladly.

I don't think Harry would object if I told you that he was not a virgin when we married, but he'd sowed his wild oats with other kinds of girls, and I was different. He thought I was special, and I agreed with him. He thought I was smarter and prettier than I am. So as long as he thought I was the kingpin, what was there to discuss? We slipped easily into what would become our life together, and everything developed naturally.

Many women are looking for love today, and I often hear from ones seeking advice about making the best of a hopeless romantic situation.

FALL IN LOVE FOR LIFE

They really do know better; they just want to hear the truth from a wise old lady. Ladies, if you are constantly wondering if somebody is "the one," it's fair to say he probably isn't.

When it's the right time and the right person, your heart will tell you. Ours did. I never went looking for a man to fall in love with. He came into my life at a time when I was ready to accept him, and we each opened up our hearts to ensure that for all we got, we gave just as much. That's the secret formula for falling in love and falling forever. You'll only land with a thump when one or both of you stop caring, stop giving, stop trying to keep your love alive.

CUTIE'S COUNSEL

1. Before getting too serious about a prospective partner, make certain the people you love and respect approve. As you start spending more time together, also make the time to socialize with these important people, as a couple.

2. When dating, even if you don't need to economize, make every third date a "no-money zone." If you find you can't have a good time without paying for the pleasure, stop dating. In hard times, you'll need compatibility to tide you over.

3. Plenty of guys know how to say all the right things to make a girl feel like a princess, but what happens when you strip away the words? If you've met "the one," he will make you feel wonderful in the quiet moments, too. Tell your man to hush for an afternoon, and find out how it feels to just be together.

HOW DO YOU KNOW?

The relationship question that people ask me more than any other is, "How did you know that Harry was the right guy for you?" (And then, sometimes, they also want to know if we went to bed together before we got married.)

I understand their interest. It's both the hardest and the easiest thing in the world to meet the right person and start a life together. I think that it's instinctive, that you know when you are comfortable with somebody. When it's the right person, he brings out the best in you, and you do the same for him.

With Harry, I felt comfortable right away, and as I got to know him better, I felt even more comfortable.

I am fortunate, because my instincts are very strong. All my life, when meeting people, I have immediately responded to an inner quality in them that I either like or I don't. If I like a person, I like him or her deeply, but if not, the person is automatically eliminated. It is an unspoken connection, very powerful, very clear. This is true of friends as well as romantic partners—and it is perhaps even more important to have this talent for picking good friends. A good friend, who is a kind and decent person who shares your values, will help you steer your life in the best direction should you ever be confused about which way to turn. Pick good friends, and everything else that's good will follow—including love. A friend who knows you well might recognize that someone is a great match for you even before you do, or see warning signs in a beau who is truly "too good to be true." A friend with good instincts is a fine person to keep around when you're weighing your romantic options, but, of course, the final decision about a partner must be your own.

Even if you don't feel as in touch with your intuition as I do, the truth is that in love and in friendship, your heart *will* tell you—if you will just let it. So many people today don't know how to hear their own hearts speaking to them. They get confused and overstimulated. They don't give their intuition the respect it deserves. If this describes you, my advice is to go someplace quiet and beautiful on a day when you don't have to be anywhere else, and to clear your mind. It might not happen right away, but don't be discouraged. Walk around, with no destination. As you get calmer, let yourself think about your relationship objectively, as something that exists in the world outside of your role in it. Examine it from all sides, and let yourself feel the feelings that come up as you explore. Are there parts of the relationship you are reluctant to examine? Are there parts that make you anxious or afraid? Are you truly interested in looking at the relationship, today and for the rest of your life? The answers will help develop your emotional intelligence, and to hear your heart when it speaks to you.

When you meet a person, and are attracted to him or her, there are so many things happening all at once. If a person makes a good impression, you might think that he or she seems like such a good match "on paper" that you ought to want to be his or her partner—even if your intuition is telling you that something is not quite right about the situation. If you are attracted physically to somebody, that can be overwhelming, but there are other types of attraction that can throw your intuition out of whack. It is just as important that you know yourself as it is to know your partner.

And to truly succeed in a love match, you must get to know your partner intimately. Not sexually, but *intimately*. Observe them in their daily life, and see how they respond to stress and aggravation. Are they gracious, or impatient? Do they make that extra effort to help other people feel safe and respected? Are they lazy, or grumpy, or irritable? People can be successful, attractive, and great conversationalists, but if they're not at home in their own skin, I promise you, they will find a way to make you feel as miserable as they do.

What's attractive is all so personal; I expect what turns me off would have been very agreeable to someone else. But those little things that set your teeth on edge are important to recognize. If it grates, the person is not for you. When people ask me how they can find the person who is right for them, I tell them that they must first understand who they are, and what it is that they are looking for.

There are things that can be brushed off. You learn to live with small imperfections. And as it happens, throughout his life Harry said the word *library* as if it were spelled *liberry*, and I could not have cared less. In fact, I grew to love it, as I loved many of his quirks, because they were the quirks of my sweetheart. Had we not been so much in love, I can easily imagine *liberry* seeming like the most irritating sound in the world.

Of course, people have different qualities that they hope to find in their ideal partner. I am a firm believer in making lists, and I think that a wonderful use of the time when you are not in a relationship is making a very specific list of the values and characteristics that make up the person you would like to spend your life with. Drawing up such a list when you are dating is dangerous, because you will inevitably give more credence to the characteristics of your current flame. You want to make a list that is true to your inner values and not the flavor of the day. And remember that it's important not to be too critical. Nobody is perfect, and if your list of requirements is too strict, you can easily overlook a person who would be very happy with you, and you with him or her. You cannot fall in love with blue eyes and perfect teeth. You have to fall in love with the character of the person.

With Harry, I saw a simple, generous person. He was truly a gentleman, and that is what I admired most about him. Everybody loved Harry. He was polite, neat, and he was always clean. He treated my family respectfully.

I would not have accepted anything else. I wouldn't have liked a guy who was critical of my family or contentious with his attitude. Although he had not received much schooling, I found Harry to be surprisingly well educated, in a natural way. He was intelligent and thoughtful, and he enjoyed reading to expand his horizons. I was attracted by how well spoken Harry was. Perhaps I was a snob, but I could not have been with somebody who used "dese," "dem," and "dose" like the brusque-talking New Yorkers I met before Harry.

As a matter of fact, when I met Harry, I was still officially in a twosome with Ira, my beau from New York City. After high school, I took a trip to see my aunts and uncles and cousins back east, and when my uncles gave me a job helping customers behind the counter in their furniture store, I stayed for some months.

I went to New York on my own because I wanted to. Also, my uncle Dave was getting married, so I could represent the California branch of the family by attending. We had come over from Egypt when I was six years old, and my family lived in New York until I was fourteen. We were real Old World Jewish immigrants, the adults selling fruit, the kids assimilating into American culture. I really felt that during my last few years in New York that I had grown up, and then *boom!* We moved to Los Angeles, and I left everything behind. At nineteen, I was hungry to see the old friends that I had grown up with, and my parents knew I'd be all right because my uncles would look after me once I arrived.

My favorite uncles, the Moscovitches, the brothers of my mother, were both wonderful, but different as could be. Irving was a very handsome man, but elegant and cool. His brother Dave was a bundle of joy. He just loved everybody, and he loved me most of all. Dave was handsome, too, only a little less handsome than Irving, and with darker hair. It was Dave who gave me my nickname, Cutie. He'd see me coming and yell across the street, "Hey, Cutie!" which would make me blush and everybody turn and stare. It's a good way for a new person to make friends in the neighborhood, getting a nickname—as long as it's a cute one and it suits you.

CHAPTER 1 :: FALLING IN LOVE

Before too long, I met Ira. He was a very lovely young man and was there when I needed a friend. He was not the first man who wanted to date me, but the couple of guys who tried, I didn't like. One of them, he thought he loved me very much, but he was certainly not for me. I don't know how other girls operate; maybe they find a lot of boys, and give each one of them a chance. Me, I eliminate—quickly! But Ira I liked immediately, and if I like, I love. I don't love very often. With him, I felt comfortable exploring the possibilities, in a very square way, because that's the kind of person I am.

Through having a job, and getting a boyfriend, I was gone much longer than I had anticipated. However, I missed my family, and so after seven months, I told Ira that I was going back home to California, and he was to follow. I explained that I could not give him a commitment until he met my family and he liked them and they liked him, too. It was very important that everybody like each other if I was going to become serious about any man.

As a going-away present, he gave me some very lovely pajamas. Had I been staying in New York, this would have been *much* too provocative a gift, but since I was going home, and he loved me, I thought it was a sweet gesture. And in those days, you were very careful not to exchange gifts in person. So the pajamas showed up very discreetly in a box, and I opened it alone, and put the pajamas on alone. No blushing or awkwardness. It was a serious gift from a serious young man. I sent him a thank-you note, of course, which I am sure I wrote while wearing my pajamas. That was about as racy as I got. Oh yes, I am a real go-to-hell kid!

Ira made plans to follow me, but he took his sweet time about it. And it was in the midst of this situation that Harry came on the scene, very innocently. Too bad for Ira, but happy for Harry and for me.

When I found him in my mother's living room that day, my intention was only to play tennis with his sister. And I am sure Harry's intention was only to play tennis with anybody, because he was a terrible tennis bum at that time. He would hang out all day at this little shop in Poinsettia Park where they sold tennis rackets, trading in his racket for a different one and trying to hit the perfect ball. (His trick was to imagine that the ball coming toward him was as big as an orange and *thwack!* He'd always hit it. Try it; you'll find that it works. And when it does, remember Harry.)

For many years afterward, we would laugh about how he thought he was getting a tennis partner that day, but he wound up with a partner for life.

It just felt so natural that we would spend more and more time together that spring. It was as if Harry had always been there, and to me that was a good sign. I liked having him around, and my parents also enjoyed him. He was a nice young man to have in the house, and ours was the kind of family that always was ready to accept someone new who fit in with our rhythms. My parents put up no barriers. They respected my opinion about this young man, and they welcomed Harry into our circle.

Sometimes, you think you have been in love, and you meet somebody else and realize—wait! No! That wasn't love at all, but *this* certainly is. All of a sudden, you find that there is someone else in the world other than the person you thought you were with, and you stop short and make a very clear evaluation of your previous association and what this new one has to offer you. That is what happened to me when Harry showed up, and as a girl who thought I had my life all sewed up, it was a real eye-opener.

Oftentimes, people will ask me if I believe in the concept of "soul mates" and if I think that Harry was mine. Certainly, I think it is remarkable that a boy born in Pennsylvania could find and fall in love with a girl born in Cairo, Egypt, after encountering one another thousands of miles away from where they started. But I also think that when we met, we were both good people who were looking for a sweet partner to fall in love with. Happily, Harry found me, but I cannot believe that if we had missed each other, we both should have been destined to live lonely lives. This is simply how our cookie crumbled, and it was a wonderful cookie.

We all like the idea of a perfect relationship and a person who is a perfect match, but that's not really how it works. Soul mates are not flawless partners. If you want to be happy in a relationship, you must learn to accept the imperfections along with all the good stuff, and stand up for the things you believe in. If you can agree with your partner on the big things, then the little troubles don't seem so important. But if you find conflict everywhere in your life together, the little things don't look so little anymore. Maybe when a couple meets and falls in love, that plants a seed, and if they are very fortunate and work hard together, in time it grows into a vine, which truly does entwine their souls together. A soul mate seems to me something that you must work to enjoy, not a connection you could just stumble onto.

So I was not looking for a soul mate when I met Harry, but simply was aware that I liked him a lot, and I imagined we might be compatible. I thought about Ira, and it seemed to me that whatever happened with me and Harry, the least I could do was to let him know that things were not quite the same as when I left New York with his pajamas under my arm. I never felt sad about breaking up with Ira, because it didn't happen until I was interested in Harry, and it only happened *because* I was interested. At that moment, I certainly did not evaluate the situation and think, "I'd better say good-bye to Ira, because I will be busy for the next seventy-three years." It was a new situation, and a pleasant one. I simply was attracted to Harry, and wanted to see what might happen if I made myself available. And very soon, he became the most important part of my life.

I thought he had lovely manners because he would constantly say, "I beg your pardon?" It was only later that I discovered that he was suffering from an injured eardrum. It had burst when, as a soldier in Hawaii, he swam out into the surf to rescue a drowning man.

So Harry's "I beg your pardon?" really meant he couldn't hear much of anything, but there was just something so charming in the way he said it. And the fact was, he did want to hear what I had to say. It's exciting to have somebody wanting to hear your words, as if you are the most interesting person in the world.

When I think back on our relationship, I remember that Harry always behaved as if he loved me, being attentive and concerned and kind. Everybody wants to be loved and admired. I certainly enjoyed the feeling of having found a guy who thought I was perfect. I knew I was perfect, and so we had a wonderful point of agreement. Or maybe neither one of us knew any better. We didn't criticize or judge each other. We decided that the other person was wonderful, and maybe coming from that positive belief, we both were careful to be *extra* wonderful so as not to disappoint the other. Harry told me early on that one thing he liked about me was that, unlike other girls he had dated, I didn't find fault in him. He wondered if I was simply keeping my criticism to myself, but the truth was, it was not my nature to look for things not to like about somebody who I found *simpatico*.

Looking back, I see that in falling in love with Harry, I was also getting to know myself: what was important to me in a love relationship and how I wanted to spend my time as a grown-up. But it was clear that I was not a playgirl looking for adventure. He knew from the start that I was only looking for a love affair that led very soon to marriage. With Harry in the picture, any interest in going out to meet new men evaporated, and my girlfriends respected that. This meant that some of my friends drifted away, while others, who were in serious relationships and could double-date, got closer. But Harry became my best friend. I guess that is what it means to grow up.

Harry was raised well enough to know that, as a young Jewish man, he must treat a young Jewish woman with the respect that he would want another man to treat his sister or his cousin. It is a form of brainwashing that all Jewish children receive. If he had tried treating me like he treated those *shiksas* from his past, getting fresh but not getting serious, I would have been more than just critical. I would have been hopping mad, and then I would have been out of the picture!

27

Honestly, I think he was bored with running around, maybe bored with having the kind of fun he had been having. You can only go to so many taxi dance halls and date so many girls you don't really care about. Harry had packed a lot of living into his young life, working hard all the time, serving in the army, moving from Pennsylvania to Hawaii to California. When we met, his big sister was married, his best friends were just getting married, and his younger sister was serious about her beau and eager to double-date with us—so it was either find a nice girl and settle down or find new friends to run around with. Lucky for him and for me, that's the time when we met.

And as for me, I was just a serious girl where romance was concerned. I could not have a casual commitment. Casual is a one-night stand of going to a party with a person, then coming home and not knowing with whom you will go to the next party. That kind of life would have made me nervous. I wanted a person with a solid background who I could count on. It was automatically ingrained in me that I wanted the feeling that homing birds have—when they seek their own and feel comfortable with another who shares a compatible disposition.

And so without either one of us talking very much about it, we settled into the groove of feeling that this is my sweetheart, and we want to spend all our free time together getting to know each other, enjoying ourselves, and seeing where these new feelings take us. Rarely would we go to the movies, because we liked to talk to each other. So anywhere we could talk, that's where you'd find us. I suppose we gossiped. We certainly talked all about our friends and our families, and ourselves. What else was there to talk about? We were simple people. I didn't have a job, and his job wasn't so interesting that it made for long conversation.

When you are young and in love and don't have a lot of money, it's always the same. You go out driving in his car; you go to the park and stroll among the flowers; you have coffee or a simple meal and linger at the table holding hands and ignoring the clock. When he does take you

home, you sit outside for as long as you can, hugging and kissing, and when you do go inside the house, you run straight to your room, climb into bed, close your eyes, and remember how his kisses felt.

If it was a Saturday night, Harry would splurge and bring me a gardenia to pin to my blouse. The smell was heavenly, and the next day I would wake up in my bedroom to the odor of jungle flowers and the memory of our big night together. For something special, we might go to Chinatown and have a full meal for twenty-five cents. Or he liked to go to the Chili Bowl, which was a diner with a round counter, and the moment you sat down, the waiter would lean in and light your cigarette. Harry still smoked then, and the attention made him laugh. We also liked McDonald's, which wasn't a chain like it is today. It had very nice food and a clean atmosphere.

Those times were so simple. I think I had three dresses, and I would rotate between them. The three dresses got a lot of wear and tear. My hair was always combed, and I wore very little makeup. It was a big deal if I put a drop of lipstick on. I did pencil my eyes, which I thought was important, coming from an Egyptian family—we know the power of a little shadow around the eyes.

Harry and I found we had the same ideas about things, even though we were so young that we didn't really have a lot of ideas.

And in our simple way we explored one another, and we learned that there was a lot to like and a lot we wanted to know better. We both knew that it was love, and it was obvious what would happen next.

CUTIE'S COUNSEL

1. To find love, you must develop good instincts and trust them. Respect your intuition. If something about a person rubs you the wrong way, pay attention, or you might be sorry later.

2. When you're not involved with a sweetheart, sit down and make a list of the qualities you'd like to find in a partner. Refer to this list when you are infatuated with someone new, and don't be afraid to reject someone who is attractive but doesn't meet your criteria. Looks fade, but shared values will last a lifetime.

3. Fill your life with trustworthy friends, and don't drop them should you fall in love. They can be your guides should you ever lose track of what is important in your life.

4. If you are interested in having a relationship, you must be available to the possibilities as they occur. Don't box yourself in or you may lose out on something special.

SETTING THE DATE

In the 1930s, when Harry and I were young, there weren't a lot of options for a couple like us, which is to say a nice Jewish girl—whose mother and father were watching closely—and boy. You either got engaged and set a wedding date or you stopped seeing each other.

Nobody dreamed of the long engagements and living together before marriage that are so common today. The reasons that couples now give for moving in together and waiting to marry—we don't have enough money to have a big wedding; we don't know each other well enough yet—would have made us laugh to hear them.

Of course, those were different times. Today, if both people are serious about each other and the relationship, it may be that living together is a good first step. Maybe you will marry; maybe not. This is a personal thing that you must decide for yourself. As long as both people respect each other and want to build a good life together, that's their business.

Society cannot judge you, but each person has standards by which he or she judges his or her own behavior. I do not like the idea behind "Why buy the cow, when you can get the milk for free?" but there is a reason that this concept has become a cliché. If you are not comfortable being intimate before marriage, you have every right to feel that way and to say, "Let's wait." If your partner does not agree, turn him or her loose so you both can find a better match.

If you are considering moving in with your sweetheart, I would advise that you only do so if you know the person very well and you both feel comfortable. You should never compromise your values for another person, no matter how fond you are of him or her, nor should you ask another person to make such a compromise. Also, I would ask any couple in this circumstance, if you are that serious about each other, why *not* get married? Is there a reason for saying no to the institution? The answer may teach you a great deal about your relationship.

But if you are on the same page, you love each other, and this is how you want to live, go for it. We live in a free country, and that means that all couples get to write their own scripts and to have a happy ending.

There's nothing wrong with you if you *can* afford to have a fancy wedding, but the important thing is that you become man and wife and begin your life together, not what kind of flowers were on the tables, the number of beads that were on the dress, nor how thick the steaks were.

And getting to know each other—wasn't that the point of marriage? Once the ceremony is over, two single people are united into one. This unified being is something new to both the bride and the groom, and each of them must get to know themselves and each other and the new life that they share. At least that's how we felt about it.

We were young people with red blood in our veins, so we were attracted to each other. But it was not an option that I would go to his apartment—the joke was that a man would ask a girl over to look at his etchings, which was a real no-no—and at my parents' home, we were closely watched. So that left his car as our most private place to be, and how private is a metal box with windows? Not very, and also not too comfortable. Perhaps that makes it easier to understand why engagements were short in our day.

So Harry and I were happily dating, and in the course of our enjoying being together so much, and recognizing that we didn't want to spend time with anybody else, we both realized that this was serious. Nobody had ever asked me to marry him before, and as it happened, Harry didn't ask me, either. He simply informed me: "Barbara, we are going to get married." And so there was no question. If he said we were getting married, we were getting married, and I was delighted to be informed of it. We picked a date that was a few months away and began to make the preparations.

First, of course, we had to go out and celebrate the occasion. My parents, Harry's sister and brother-in-law, and Harry and I went out to a fancy Hollywood nightclub, where to my amusement my father told the waiter that, yes, the young lady had his permission to have a cocktail. It was the start of my grown-up life, my life with Harry, and I enjoyed it very much—although I never have developed a taste for cocktails. My idea of a good drink is a mudslide, which tastes so delicious that I don't notice the alcohol at all. I would just as soon have a milk shake.

But even before I knew that Harry wanted to marry me, my father was let in on the secret. Harry went to my father, with bankbook in hand, and asked if it would be acceptable if he were to marry his daughter. At the time, Harry had saved one hundred sixteen dollars, which was not bad. And his boss had said if Harry were to marry, he would get a raise of five dollars a week, which made it twenty-seven dollars. My father looked at the bankbook, looked at Harry, thought for a moment, and said yes, he could have me. My father could tell that we loved each other, and he saw that Harry could support me and that he was a mensch, so why not?

As it happened, one of the first things that Harry asked me to do with him was to be his partner at the wedding of his (and soon mine as well) dear friends, Jimmy and Marie Leonetti. Harry was actually living with the Leonetti boys, so Jimmy's marriage meant a change in Harry's home situation.

I knew right away that I wanted to go to this wedding and share a romantic experience with Harry. It was a very do-it-yourself kind of wedding, with no pretense. They were such nice kids. You never felt Marie was critical of you, and Jimmy was a very fine man. Somebody played

FALL IN LOVE FOR LIFE

the concertina. The simple table was set by Jimmy's brother Mike. They had wine; they had salami; they had pickles. Marie was a very good cook when she had the money to cook with, but they were just starting out, and they made a beautiful wedding together.

I guess that it made a big impression on him, that his friends were settling down together, because within just a few months, we were headed down that road ourselves. My father had a friend who was a jeweler, so we got a deal on the ring. I am sure it did not hurt that Jimmy and Marie liked me, and I them. And not long after that, Harry's younger sister, Lil, decided to marry her beau, Leo Steinberg, who was a very nice, substantial young man. I like to think we had a little to do with that.

It all just goes to show how important it is that two people come together at the right time for each of them to make a real commitment to one another. If either person is feeling wishy-washy about romance, that's it; the romance will go down the drain. But both Harry and I were in the position to explore the possibilities, and we did so. I was twenty, which at the time was not unusually young to get married. We grew up faster than kids do today. I looked at Harry and I thought, "Yes, I want to marry an older man." Five years difference isn't that much older, but it was old enough for me. As for life experience, he had already been in the service and, with Jimmy and Marie's marriage, had recently taken his own apartment. So he was more sophisticated about what the world had to offer than I was at the time.

And he was working, which in the Depression was not a trivial thing. Harry was such a hard worker; I knew I could safely go from my parents' house to his home without fear. Harry always liked to use the expression "the Cooper Luck," because whatever we stuck our necks out for, we didn't stick them out too far, and if we did, we were able to handle it. We never went bankrupt, neither did we make a lot of money, but there was always enough for what we needed and what we wanted for ourselves and for our children.

I don't think of it as luck. To me it is just the Jewish word, *beshert*, or it is meant to be. We were meant to be comfortable, thank God. We simply were ourselves. We had our heads on right, no illusions of grandeur, just happy to be ourselves, doing what we were supposed to do. So Harry was Harry, and I was myself, and together we were something new. We liked how we were together, so we made it official.

CUTIE'S COUNSEL

1. If you're serious about one another, it's fine to get married quickly. Maybe not as quickly as we did, but don't feel you must have a long engagement just because it's fashionable.

2. Marriage is contagious, and so is monogamy. If you would like to have a partner and a happy home, surround yourself with people on the same path.

3. Although it is tempting to spend all your time with a new beau, make the effort to get to know his friends, too. If your sweetheart has nice friends, that speaks well for his character, and since you will eventually want to go back out into the social world, it will help if you find his people agreeable.

RECITING THE VOWS

In 1937 America, we didn't have a wedding culture like there is today. There were no bridal magazines for me to buy, nobody in my circle had ever compiled a registry, and if you had asked us about our color scheme, table favors, or what flavors of cake filling we wanted, we would have stared at you in utter confusion.

Basically, a 1930s wedding was a big deal, but not *that big* a deal. And it was something that we, as the bride and groom, certainly participated in, but not something we worked on as a project.

Once we started the ball rolling by getting engaged, it was really a simple thing, strolling down the road together to the wedding ceremony. In my family, although we weren't very religious, it was expected that you would marry in a house of God, that the guests would dress up in their finest outfits, that there would be music and entertainment, and we would all share a lovely meal.

But as for the planning, what did I know about throwing an elegant affair? When you are twenty years old and first leaving the house, your parents take over. Or, in my case, my father took over, and I was happy to have him do so. Believe me, *nobody* would have been happy had I questioned him.

My father, Louis, was an Eastern European gentleman, very charming, very demanding. He was born in Kherson, Russia (in what is now Ukraine), and started his professional life in the commercial quarter of

Cairo, Egypt, where he was a merchant. So he made his living on his wits and his charisma. A real wheeler-dealer. When we came to Los Angeles via New York, he worked his way up, first running a yard on Sunset Boulevard selling secondhand car tires, then in the discount retail shoe business, a trade that Harry and I would follow in.

At the time of our marriage, my father still had the tire yard, but he also had a stroke of good luck. In October 1936, he was one of the preliminary winners of the Irish Hospital Sweepstakes, a lottery tied to a horse race. His ticket on Noble King brought the family almost three thousand dollars (worth almost fifty thousand dollars in today's money), and when he heard that Harry and I were to be married, he wasted no time in planning a wonderful party for all his friends and business associates. It was still the Depression, and we did not spend lavishly, but within our means, it was quite an affair.

What did I care? I didn't know any better. I was happy I was in love and getting married to a man who loved me. Meanwhile, my father was having a ball selecting the menu, compiling the guest list, choosing the venue, and so on.

In those days, the young couple just had to show up. Maybe it wouldn't be such a bad thing if it were still that way. In my capacity as an advice maven, I often hear from engaged couples who are arguing with their families about who is in charge of the wedding, who is going to pay for it, which person gets to decide on all the important factors, how many guests can come. It can so easily become a huge headache, and the important thing— the fact that it is a union of two people in love with each other—gets lost in all the minutiae.

It makes me think I was fortunate that all I had to worry about was my dress and my hair, and remembering my lines under the *chuppah* (the Jewish wedding canopy). As for writing our own vows, such a thing was unheard of. We went along with the regular vows, and they were the standard ones, not so unusual that I would remember them. Whatever the rabbi said was what we had, the standard thing at a traditional Jewish wedding—not orthodox, just ordinary Jewish, like us.

I was happy with my dress, which was white satin and very pretty. I loved my flowers. But my hair, oh! Somebody convinced me that to get married, of course I must have a special hairdo, so I went to the hair salon and let the girl do her thing. When I looked in the mirror, I almost *plotzed*. Usually, I wore my hair very simply, in natural waves to my shoulders. I was used to my own pretty, simple hair, not this stiff concoction. It just wasn't me. Instead of letting this ruin my day, I went straight home, washed my hair, and set it the way I liked it. I'm sure Harry would have thought I looked gorgeous either way, but there was no way I was going to get up in front of God and everybody with my hair feeling like a porcupine's spines, and looking nearly as prickly.

Now you must understand that I occupied a very special position within my family. I was the oldest child, very close to my parents, and my marriage was the first for our immediate family since we left Egypt in the 1920s. My father had been waiting all his life for a chance to show off his daughter and his skills as an American host.

September 18, 1937, was the big day.

First, we had the proper marriage ceremony in the local temple, which was the one we contributed to, although, as I said, we were not very religious. It was very simple and very beautiful, with the exciting conclusion when Harry stomped on the glass to break it.

And for Harry and me, it would have been enough if that was all we did. But for my father, it was only the beginning of the celebration. From there, we moved to the secular part of the affair, the party at the White House Café, on Wilshire Boulevard.

We had about 130 guests, and I knew maybe a dozen of them. Harry and I didn't have so many friends, my family was small, and most of his people were still back east. But, of course, we invited everybody that his local family felt was important in his life.

Mainly, it was a party for my father and his business associates, and they all had a wonderful time. They feasted, and danced, and reminisced about their own weddings, and they ogled the belly dancers and the sword swallowers, who were the main attraction. Leave it to my father to turn his daughter's wedding into a traveling carnival show. As for Harry, he was busy enjoying his T-bone steak. And then, at one point, they must have picked me up in a chair, which is part of the fun of doing the Jewish wedding dance routine—though rather unnerving for the poor person in the chair.

On the drive to our hotel room after midnight, Harry told me that he felt like he was the king, and on top of the world. Taking me away from my father was a manly ritual, very formal and old-fashioned. Harry had missed out on so much of being part of a Jewish family after losing his mother in the flu epidemic of 1918 and not living with his father as he was growing up, but now he was filling in those gaps by playing the role of the dutiful husband. Although my father paid for the party, Harry proudly paid for the marriage itself, handing two dollars to the rabbi and gaining a joke he would enjoy for the rest of our lives together: now he could tell anyone who asked about our love affair that he had bought me, and I came very cheaply at that!

It seemed to Harry and me that every single person there, in the course of wishing us luck and congratulations, made the same remark: we were so little and so cute that we looked just like the figures on top of the wedding cake. So maybe we did, but once the party ended, we were ready to wipe the frosting off our feet and get on with the exciting business of beginning our lives together.

1. When making decisions about your wedding ceremony, if your reason for doing something a certain way is basically materialistic, reconsider. There are things in your life worth counting coins over, but the symbols of your love for each other should be pure. A simple wedding, planned and accomplished with love, is more moving than a fancy affair meant to impress the neighbors.

2. If people who love you want to take over planning aspects of your wedding, think about letting them do so. It means less work for you and more happiness for them—and what really matters is that you are married, not that you planned the ceremony down to the color of your groomsmen's socks. If somebody wishes to take all that headache over for you, let them—and plan your honeymoon instead.

3. Traditions got to be traditional for a reason. Don't be too modern in your marriage ceremony and miss out on a potentially powerful experience.

Mr. and Mrs. Louis Prupis
request the honour of your presence
at the marriage of their daughter

Barbara

to

Mr. Harry Cooper

on Saturday, the eighteenth day of September
at seven thirty p. m.

Haskell's Whitehouse Cafe

637 South Ardmore Avenue

at Wilshire

Los Angeles, Calfornia

R. S. V. P.
516½ No. Spaulding Ave.
Los Angeles, California

Chapter 2: **MAKING A MARRIAGE**

AFTER THE ALTAR

And just like that, Harry and I were man and wife. Looking back, it was all quite the whirlwind. It was only five months since I had come home to California to see what the next phase of my life would look like, and in that time I had met this lovely fellow, set my New York boyfriend free, and embarked on a grand adventure.

Up until the wedding hour, I had enjoyed every moment that I spent with my Harry—but he was really still a stranger to me. We had never spent a night together, so I didn't know what he looked like first thing in the morning—cute, as it happens—and *he* didn't know how crabby I can be if you wake me up before I'm ready. But what we both knew was that we were thrilled to be embarking on this life together, and quite prepared to be a little shocked by real life as it intruded into our up-till-then "perfect" romance.

First on the agenda was a honeymoon trip, and lucky for us, we lived in Los Angeles, so we had a great many resorts to chose from, from the desert to the sea. For our first night together, we stayed in the aptly named Constance Hotel in Pasadena, and from there we headed for the mountains. We selected a hotel by the lake in Big Bear, mostly because my father, through one of his business associates, found us a deal.

Even though it was only one hundred miles from Los Angeles, this was a remote part of America. We knew nothing about life in the mountains or what to do there, but we packed our playclothes, and Harry's bow and arrow, and up we went. He was keen on archery and thought it would be fun to run through the woods playing hunter.

Also, at the last minute, I had grabbed our tennis rackets and the Sunday paper, because the thought of walking up to a hotel desk clerk with a young man by my side, both of us holding suitcases that did not match, seemed too scandalous. So what if he was my husband? Remember, I was very young and not very sophisticated. I didn't know we could just walk into a hotel, pay the bill, and get a room key. I was sure that they were whispering, "Oh, would you look at that racy young couple! Shame on them!"

So my little hope was that when they saw the tennis rackets and the archery equipment, they would think that our interest was not in sex; it was mostly in sports. Today, of course, I would say "Who cares what they think?" And I am sure that they didn't think anything at all, since we were just one more blushing honeymoon pair among hundreds, as far as they were concerned.

And this is where we started our life as man and wife. What happened in our hotel room is what happens in most hotel rooms when two young people spend their first few nights together. We were eager to go to bed with one another, and that is part of the reason that we married so quickly. Happily, we found that we were compatible here, just as we were in our everyday life. And although I was very shy and self-conscious when we checked in to our honeymoon hotel, by the time we were packing up our unused tennis rackets and a newspaper filled with information I could not report to you, I felt like a grown-up married lady. Then off we went, back down the mountain to Los Angeles, where a new life awaited us.

We were both so excited. It was an adventure just being together. When you are honeymooning, all of a sudden you have a license to sleep with a man, the person who loves you, who is the person you love. We didn't need to jump out of an airplane to get our thrills. Just the excitement of our simple little life was plenty.

Maybe we were square, but what should I tell you—we found this exciting. It *was* exciting, to have our first apartment. It was exciting to sit down to our first meals together. It was exciting to burn the toast. We laughed a lot.

When I think back on our early life together, it all boils down to the basics: we were either cleaning house, or kissing, or fighting, or cooking. If we didn't have something important to do, maybe we would go to a movie. Remember, we had no television. Radio, we had it, but we were not obsessed. Harry and I would listen to the serials together, or a story about life on other planets. It was the closest to theater that we had early on. This was a little something to look forward to from one week to another.

But mostly, we would talk. He would tell me about his day at work: problems with his deliveries, a funny thing his boss had said, something unusual he saw on the street while driving. And I would fill him in on everything happening in the neighborhood: what was at the market, what our neighbor said, all about a movie I did not see but somebody told me about. Everyday talk, nothing important, but it made us feel as if we had spent our day together instead of apart. Before too long, we made sure that we had a way to work together, too, because we found we were one of those couples who is happier without much time spent apart.

A good marriage is one without much conflict and strife, but it is unreasonable to expect that two young people will be able to avoid these flare-ups without working at it. The most important thing for any couple trying to get along is to think before you speak. If you are bickering and find you are getting angry, take a deep breath and change course, and ask your partner to do the same. Try saying something conciliatory, like "I don't know why this is making me so upset, but it is, so can you just humor me and help me get over it?" By simply admitting you are losing your cool, you may find that the anger quickly dissipates.

Oftentimes, like a fire, a small fight can be extinguished easily, but if it's allowed to grow, *watch out!* So should you become upset, do not let it escalate. Stop the conversation and go do something else on your own, preferably something physically demanding so you don't have time to brood. Smart couples agree that when either one of them asks for a time-out, that request shall always be granted.

Maybe you are a fighter outside the home, at work or school or with political causes, but with your beloved, you should know you are on the same side and that small disagreements do not change that fact. Marriage is a combination of understanding, feeling comfortable with the other person, and loving to be with him or her. If you have that, you can weather any conflict that should come along.

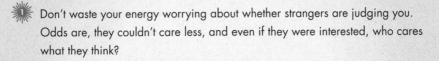

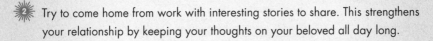

CUTIE'S COUNSEL

1. Don't waste your energy worrying about whether strangers are judging you. Odds are, they couldn't care less, and even if they were interested, who cares what they think?

2. Try to come home from work with interesting stories to share. This strengthens your relationship by keeping your thoughts on your beloved all day long.

3. If you are bickering and find you are both getting really upset, take a deep breath and change course, and ask your partner to do the same.

KEEPING HOUSE

When Harry and I began our life together, there were so many things that were new and exciting and a bit frightening. Neither one of us had ever decorated a home, or even had the responsibility of deciding the basics of our living environment. I was coming straight from my parents' house, where my mother, nicknamed the Duchess, had crafted an elegant, welcoming domestic space for her family and our guests. And Harry had lived with many different people—extended family, fellow soldiers, male friends—fitting into the environment he found without making any waves of his own. Always a guest, but never before the host.

So looking at the blank walls of our first apartment was a big shock to us both. Instead of the built-up assemblage of decades of family life, here was a clear indication that we were on our own and needed to make the important decisions that would shape our surroundings and represent that elusive thing—*home*—for our children, when they arrived.

Our first apartment was small, just the basics that we needed to survive. We had a bedroom, a living room, and a kitchen. Although this was California and not New York, I would categorize our first home as tenement living. There were other people all around us, and we had to pass through nondescript public spaces in order to get to our equally underwhelming private ones.

After our honeymoon, we got right down to business—or rather, Harry did. He got up in the morning and went off to work in his truck all day long. Not me. I did not have a job, nor did I qualify for a job. My uncles had been kind to employ me in New York, but I had no uncles to turn to in Los Angeles. And anyway, the thinking of the time was that a married lady would not work outside the home.

Harry went away five days a week and left me there alone. I was no longer the girl who lived in her parents' house and could do as she pleased. This little space was mine to command, and with it came responsibilities.

Honestly, I didn't know what to do with myself. Then, as now, I enjoyed daydreaming, and that's how I spent a big chunk of my day. If I had an errand to run, I'd run it slowly, to kill time. Back in our apartment, I would attempt to clean and decorate, but I really didn't know how to begin. I am ashamed to admit that I was bored, and like I always say, "If you're bored, you're boring."

If I could go back and visit my younger self, I would push her out the door and tell her, "Don't come home until you've had an adventure! You are a young woman in a wonderful town. Go to the art museum; take a class; visit a girlfriend. You ought to be struggling to choose what to do today, not killing the hours like they were flies. Before you know it, you'll have children and wish you had so much free time at your disposal!"

Well, with time I learned how to take advantage of what life had to offer, and I began my lifelong relationship with my best friends aside from Harry, the books that lived in the public library. And I learned a little trick so that I would never be bored: when I was almost too busy to think, I would still take a moment to write down the things I would love to do if I only had the time. Then, when free time presented itself, I did not run the danger of being unable to think of something to do, since I had a list to consult.

My primary memory of that first home was that the landlady employed men to care for the premises. I remember them well because of their habit of unlocking our apartment door, peering in at me, shaking their heads, and shutting the door. Although they were always very polite and never did anything else, it was scary, I was not used to it, and I didn't know how to react.

I realize now that they were probably concerned because I was being so terribly quiet, and they just wanted to make sure somebody was still alive in there. I didn't have neighbors to visit with, I didn't have children, and I guess I didn't have the sense to keep the radio going. So they would just open up the door to see if everything was under control. Also, I expect the landlady was concerned that this silly kid might burn the house down if she tried to bake a loaf of bread. Today I wouldn't stand for such an intrusion, but I was a different person then.

Later, after I had my kids, I had some run-ins with the landlady. Her name was Mrs. Zid, and her way of keeping house was not the same as mine. In those days, you had to boil diapers to sterilize them. I would cook them on the stove in the kitchen, then hang them on the line to dry. Well, Mrs. Zid would come through the entry hall with a rag, dusting the leaves on the houseplants. Very nice. But then, always, she would touch my clean white diapers with her dusty fingers. And because of her, I became neurotic. I didn't want *anyone* touching my babies' diapers. So when Harry came home, I would vent about this, but there was not a lot I could do. It was hard to find a nice apartment. You took the good with the bad.

But maybe I was too lax with my housekeeping in other ways. When my father would visit, no matter how hard I tried to make things perfect, he would invariably find some spot with dust on it, run his finger through it, and say, "What, there wasn't time to dust the furniture?" I guess that's one way of saying "I love you."

Honestly, I think my way of running a household was funny. I am not the most organized person. I would sweep one room out completely but somehow not get to the other one. If it was the hottest day of the year, that was the day I selected to do the windows, and I would moan, groan, and scarcely finish the job. Sometimes I would laugh at my own mistakes, but I was smart enough not to share all of them with Harry when he came home. Better he not know what a silly goose he had married.

Coming into the marriage, I confess that my basic philosophy of housekeeping was to do as little as possible. Make your bed, put the dishes in the sink, and go to bed!

Well, of course, I could not get away with doing so little. So I tried to be a good little housewife. But, oh, I did not like it. Dusting. Do you know that you have to do it every day? If you do not, the dust will just come back, cling to itself, and then it's not dust; it's dirt. When you look at some adorable little tchotchke in the store and think, "I like it, but that will only collect dust," then you know you are a housewife.

You must sweep the floor every day, and if somebody spills something on the floor, then you must wash it. The bedding must be clean. The windows must be done, eventually. You must keep the refrigerator clean because there are always leftovers to put inside it, and these leftovers must go inside clean jars, which you store for a while, then throw away.

That's housekeeping. Very monotonous. You never can rest, or it gets away from you. But you have to keep the house neat so you can live in it, and not be a slob, and I did so.

Happily, Harry was not critical of me, nor was he a mess maker. He accepted the home as I kept it, and really, he said very little. Mostly, "Barbara, I love you," and "Barbara, you are beautiful." To know you would hear such things at the end of the day made it a little easier to wash his socks and scrub the pots and pans with a smile.

But, eventually, I found my secret weapon: Maggie, marvelous Maggie. After we'd been married a few years, we had a little extra money, so we gave it to Maggie. For twenty years, once a week, she took care of our home and helped with our children. It was nice to have somebody pleasant I could count on; and all the tasks I was not good at, she performed with ease. This gave me the time to focus on my children and my husband and myself, which was a very great gift. I loved her, and because I loved her, Harry loved her, too.

And after Maggie moved on to new adventures, we found Mr. Hill. He was just what every family wants—a good man, a very good man. He was renowned for his floors and his windows—the cleanest in town—so, thanks to Mr. Hill, that was what *I* was known for. And the wonderful thing about windows is that once they are done, they are usually good for a month. And thanks to these wonderful people, everything was picked up and put away where it belonged, at least in the front of the house, where a neighbor or my parents might see, and all the things that could shine shined.

I always said thank you to Maggie and Mr. Hill and told everyone how terrific they were, but I bet they never imagined that ordinary little Barbara Cooper would praise them in a book. I wish I could go back and tell them, and we would share a laugh.

When you work hard, the temptation is to come home and just *plotz* (which is Jewish for "relax," or maybe "die," depending on the context)— to throw your dirty clothes on the floor or hide a mess behind closet doors. This is not a new story. What *is* new since I was a bride is that now both husband and wife probably work outside the home and are equally tired at the end of the day.

And still, many women write to me complaining that they end up doing all the household chores, with no real help from their partners. The fact of the matter is that very few people enjoy physical labor, and even for those who like to work up a sweat, cleaning up a house is hardly on their list of exciting activities. But a house needs to be kept tidy, and not every family can afford a housekeeper. Partners need to remember that they are in this life together and to both pull their weights when it comes to keeping house. I suggest trying a little flattery: tell your sweetheart that you have chores to do, but you are conflicted because what you *really* want is to spend time with him. Also, you can remind him that once the chores are done, there will be time for more important things, like making love!

In our home, I did the day-to-day things, but I could always count on Harry to help out when asked. Maybe we would fold the clothes together and talk about our respective days, or I'd give him the feather duster and point up at the places that were too high for me to reach. If I was cooking dinner, he might make the salad, not because he was so interested in salads, but as an excuse to be together. And whenever we had a big project, like painting walls, moving rugs, or flipping the mattress, of course he was front and center with his work togs on, and I was his assistant.

If housekeeping is a source of arguments in your house, the best advice I can give you is to cut back somewhere else and find the money for at least occasional maid service. This was the smartest money we ever spent, and I think you will agree if you give it a try.

Well, once I discovered the secret of having help in the home, we were sitting pretty. Aside from books, which were always piled willy-nilly on every surface, we enjoyed a well-kept home, and that made it so much easier to enjoy, and to entertain. My job was relegated to the superficial chores, like putting dirty dishes into soapy water in the sink. Nobody had dishwashers in those days, at least nobody I knew. But even a halfhearted housekeeper like me could clear and soak the dishes, or throw the dirty linen in the clothes hamper. And once the dishes had soaked, they were a pleasure to clean. Or as close to a pleasure as cleaning a dish can be!

I will let you in on the secret, whether you have help in the house or not: don't leave things sitting around, but take them to the place where they are one step closer to being clean and put away. If you can remember to pick up after yourself, it makes things so much easier. I have to remind myself. I forget. But look around at the mess you've made, and you'll remember soon enough.

What I discovered was that if you don't have dirty dishes and dirty pots and pans, you haven't got a problem. If your floor is swept, hooray! And with the hard work under control, that meant I was not so crabby, and Harry and I could begin to enjoy the good parts about keeping a house together.

Do you think the prince and princess of fairy-tale days argued about whose turn it was to take the garbage out? Of course not. They, like Harry and I, argued about such important matters as metallic wallpaper, yea or nay?

And should the artwork in the main part of the house be more feminine or more masculine? Antiques or the fashion of the day? And is it worth spending a little more for a pretty stove when the clunky old stove we've got still works? There was never an argument when it came to the garbage: that's a man's job!

It took us quite a while to get into the groove of what we wanted our home to be like. For young people starting out, the onus is on just you two to create a welcoming space to live in. When two people come together, from their parents' homes or from their own living spaces, it's not always the case that they will see eye to eye on how their surroundings should look and make them feel. There are as many different options as there are individual tastes and styles, and the atmosphere that makes one person happy can leave his or her partner feeling like a visitor in a strange land.

The secret is to figure out what will make you both deliriously happy or, at the very least, to find the environment that you can both live with and that doesn't break the bank. Although there are few things as important as feeling comfortable at home, this can be a topic that is completely overlooked when it comes to talking about your future together.

Perhaps one of you has very strong opinions about interior decoration and the proper layout of furnishings, and the other one thinks it's wise to simply stand back and let the person with the big ideas make all the decisions. That will only work if your partner's taste is to your own, or if you are that rare person who really doesn't care about your environment.

Besides, I think that decorating together is great fun. It gives a couple something new to talk about, and it's hard to beat the satisfaction of completing a creative project together. Today, there are many wonderful books and websites dedicated to teaching any nincompoop who comes along how to look at a blank white box and see all the possibilities. When we were starting out, it was not so simple. Yes, there were books about homemaking and decoration, but they were quite wordy, with just a few black-and-white drawings illustrating the proper swag of a curtain, how far your dining room table ought to be from the credenza, or the proper setting of a luncheon table. The recommended styles were quite formal and mature—and expensive, too.

We tried to be more playful in our decorating, and if the results were not always beautiful, we enjoyed ourselves. DIY is nothing new. In the 1940s there was also some interest in being crafty, and I fell for the fad. Harry was very tolerant of my experiments as I slopped antique white paint all over our wooden icebox and an old bedroom set. I thought that I could paint in those days, but I was not very meticulous. As to whether it came out perfectly, I can tell you it did not. But if I knew the difference, I didn't let on, and Harry was polite enough to tell me he thought it all looked very *clean.* So that was my attempt, and we lived with it for a while.

Then, when Harry became the crafty one, always cooking up some cockamamie contraption in his garage workshop, I was equally tolerant and polite about the results. Maybe the things we made were not perfect, but we thought the people making them were wonderful. The smartest thing Harry ever made also tells you a lot about our relationship in recent years. It was a portable magazine holder, comprised of bent coat hangers and elastic, which fit over the steering wheel of our car and was meant to hold an issue of *National Geographic.* It was not beautiful, but it did the job. With this doodad at hand, we would drive to the mall, where Harry would sit in the sun reading about polar exploration and the planets, while I shopped in Ross Dress for Less. That was a perfect outing for us both.

My advice to young couples starting out is to get on the same page about how they're going to live in their home. Communicate. Find a comfortable middle ground on matters of neatness, formality, and style. And if you do not agree that everything should be the same, think how lucky you are if you have more than one room in which to live, and ensure that both halves of your pair have a place where they can do things *their* way.

In our family, this meant that Harry always had his garage for puttering in, and I was permitted to make the master bath as girlish as I liked—which was very girlish, indeed. On other matters, we communicated and comfortably compromised, and made a home that we very much enjoyed living in, and where our family and guests always felt welcome.

CUTIE'S COUNSEL

✳ If a dirty house is the root of your household arguments, find room in your budget for maid service. It is surprisingly affordable considering how much stress it dissolves away.

✳ When mooning about how wonderful life will be when you are married, don't neglect to talk about the practical aspects of how you'd like to live life day-to-day. Nothing has a bigger impact on a couple's happiness, yet it's often overlooked.

✳ The time for having singularly strong opinions is when you are a single person. Once you choose to be one-half of a pair, you must compromise, so that no one person gets what he or she wants at the expense of the other. It may take some getting used to, but reaching decisions that you both can live with can be quite romantic, since each one is a symbol of your connection.

BURNING THE TOAST

Poor Harry. Here he was in his little apartment home with his cute little wife in her cute little apron, standing in her cute little kitchen, and blinking like a little lost lamb. And it was in this kitchen that I tried to cook, but oh, I was never a cook. I didn't fool Harry, but I didn't try to fool him either. I said, "My dear, you married a very nice girl who does not know how to cook," and that I would try, but that I wasn't sure if I was capable.

The first tragedy of the noncook is to try and please her husband with breakfast. I attempted to make some kind of hot cereal. How hard could it be—boiling water, oats, a little salt and sugar? Well, he sat down at the table, and I came to him, so proud, holding out this bowl of goop I had prepared with all the love in my heart.

He tasted it, made an awful face, and pushed the bowl away.

It was so bad that even Harry, who complained about nothing, could not pretend he liked it. And that was enough for me to break down in tears. So I cried, and after he left the house, I tasted that cereal, and then I cried all over again. It really *was* that bad. The cereal I figured out eventually, but I never was what you would call a real cook. However, I did learn the tricks to presenting an adequate, pleasing meal on a pretty table, and there were not too many more mornings that ended in tears—at least not over the cereal!

CHAPTER 2 :: MAKING A MARRIAGE

When we were very young, we lived on a strict budget. We had between us just one vehicle, the truck that Harry used to make his deliveries, and in the 1930s, men did not help with the grocery shopping. So while Harry was at work, I would walk to the market with my allotment of cash for our groceries.

Once I was there, I had to decide what we could afford, how much I could carry, what I could do with these items, and how to make them stretch through the day or the week. I quickly learned that apples, onions, and potatoes are all very heavy, but that heavy things don't go bad quickly. I learned to be friendly with the butcher, who could tell me what was fresh and what the best deals were. And, most important, I learned how to balance a budget, which would be crucial when Harry and I went into business on our own.

I wasn't a big spender. Once I had to decide whether I would buy ink to write a letter or clothespins, and, ultimately, I decided to buy the ink. I can't remember when I last bought either one of those things.

I think that if young people had to carry their groceries home on foot today, it would do a lot to combat obesity and food waste, too. The French, who are my favorite people after those who live in Los Angeles, know all about this clever way of shopping. Of course, it's easier if you live walking distance from good stores.

This was my job, to keep house and feed my family. And we ate. We didn't starve. Plus, on Sundays, my parents invited us to dinner, so we could always count on at least one proper meal prepared with a bit more flair than I could muster—and leftovers for Monday night. Both of my parents were confident in the kitchen. My mother's specialty was something she called "Russell Stew," featuring very thinly sliced meat, ground onions, and a few carrots, with flour to thicken the gravy. She watched it for hours. Her stew was simple but very flavorful. And every couple of years my father decided to make boiled *kreplach*, an Eastern European dumpling that you can stuff with cheese or cherries or mashed quince fruits. These were not things I cooked at home, but I enjoyed these family favorites at their table.

Let me share with you my philosophy of how to serve a meal. I think it is important to serve several courses and to spread the dining experience out so that the family can enjoy their food, and one another. So in my household you would not find a five-minute dinner consisting only of a pizza pie or chicken legs—and not just because I can't stand chicken! Every night we would start with basically the same salad: lettuce, tomatoes, radishes, cucumbers, and green onions, with a simple dressing. (Really this was an excuse for me to get my ration of radishes, a great favorite that others in my family have not always enjoyed as much as I have. Did you know they are delicious with a little smear of butter? I learned that from my grandmother, who learned it from her grandmother.)

Then we would have some meat, because in those days, your husband would ask, "What is this?" if you tried to serve him an evening meal with no meat. We all knew we had to get our protein, even if we didn't know much about vitamins, calories, carbohydrates, and so forth. Somehow, we did survive, and most people looked and felt pretty good.

To my pleasure, and to Harry's, I became a skilled short-order cook. I might make lamb chops, a hamburger sandwich, maybe a cutlet. Never liver, because my family made it clear that if I made liver, it would sit on the plate and wait for me to eat it. And, of course, a potato, because what is your meat without a potato on the side? But as long as you have a beginning, a middle, and an end to your meal, you are in business.

At our table we did not serve soda pop. For our children, there would be water, milk, or juice. And for the adults, usually coffee. No wine. That was not our habit, and although I have read about how you can combine this wine with that entrée, this information did not affect me at all. I never have tried to be something I am not.

CHAPTER 2 :: MAKING A MARRIAGE

But if we went to a friend's house and were served wine, we might try it. I know that it is not considered a gourmet item, but I do like Manischewitz, the sweet Jewish wine, so if that is available, yes, you can pour me a glass.

The funny thing is that for many years, new friends who did not know me yet would bring to our house a bottle of liquor. And unless they drank it all during the party they attended, this liquor would go straight to the back of my cupboard. I had no use for it, but it would be rude not to accept or keep the bottle. So they piled up, and we even moved them from house to house, and many years later, my grandchildren, who were learning to enjoy cocktails, would find rare vintages hidden away and get very excited. So, eventually, these hostess gifts paid off, just not as intended.

At the end of my dinners, we would have a modest dessert, rarely anything fancy. Jell-O pudding or cookies; sometimes just a cupcake. Or you could go to the store and come home with a box of ice cream, which in those days we served with a knife, not a spoon. We opened the box all the way out on the cutting board and cut the ice cream into slabs for everybody at the table. Nothing went back into the freezer. The great favorite to keep arguments down was Neapolitan, which is rows of chocolate, vanilla, and strawberry in the same box. Try it; your family will enjoy it, too.

And that was our dinner for many years.

However, on Friday night, we would be more Jewish, which meant I would put some gefilte fish on the table, even though I could not stand to eat it. But for some reason, my husband liked this substance, which I would describe as a *gelatinous dumpling made of carp.* Yes, really. And it was a tradition, so I would open the jar while holding my breath and serve it to my family, being very careful to set it down at Harry's end of the table. I was lucky to live in the twentieth century, when gefilte fish could be purchased in a jar. Just a few decades earlier, women would bring home a live fish and store it in the bathtub until they were ready to cook.

In keeping with the Jewish theme, for soup we would have a borscht, either cabbage borscht or beet, with some chuck meat cooked in the pot.

And maybe for a side dish, noodle kugel, which is sweetened pasta that's halfway between a pudding and a casserole. And sometimes, for a special breakfast, I would make fried matzo, which is like French toast, but using the unleavened matzo cracker in place of the bread. We also loved potato pancakes, or latkes, but I used raw potato, not boiled like some people do. This type of meal was a great favorite of my husband's, and although we were never very religious, we enjoyed sharing the Jewish food traditions with our children.

Harry was a good eater, and it was easy to please him. If he had been more critical, we might not have been so happy, since my cooking was adequate but never gourmet. There is a legend that Jewish mothers are all wonderful cooks, but in my experience, this is an exaggeration. People are people, and they're either interested in the kitchen or they're not. So if you were looking for the Cordon Bleu service or what Mrs. Astor would serve, you should visit another house. But nobody ever left my table hungry or with the feeling he or she had been ignored.

If Harry was ever unhappy with his meal, after that awful incident with the cereal, he never was so cruel as to let on. Sometimes I would make a serious blunder, and the entire meal would be a disaster bound straight for the garbage can. When that did happen, my sweet husband would say something to make me laugh, and we would get into the car and go out for hamburgers without another word.

Making food for your family is a primal, motherly act, and it does feel bad when you fail in that regard. I have always been grateful that my husband quickly learned that to criticize a dish served with love would be a very big faux pas. I am not a chef, and my family members are not restaurant critics—we are just Mama and the people she loves. Every meal, whatever it tastes like, is equally good from that perspective!

We both loved to eat, so when possible, I would try to cook something a little special. Harry always liked it if I made him tri-tip, which is a cut of meat that tastes very good but is not too expensive. So that I liked! And with this we would have a special salad, meaning I would include a few olives. Pickles would be on the table in a bowl, and some flowers in a vase, and to punch up the potato, it would be prepared with cheese and onions. Funny how such little things made the whole evening seem like a grand affair. This would be for occasions like a birthday or if one of the children brought home a good report card.

Sometimes the treat did not go over so well. Once, early in our marriage, I remember telling Harry that we would be having something special for dessert. Of course, I was not foolish enough to attempt to bake for him. Instead I went to the bakery and bought a little, six-inch pie, which I thought we would have that night after dinner. As I sat in the apartment all day waiting for Harry to come home, the pie was calling to me. Eventually I went over and took a very small sliver, just to see what it was like. What it was like was *wonderful*, so later on, I took another small sliver. Before I knew what I had done, one-third of the pie was gone, or really closer to one-half—it was not a large pie to begin with.

I looked at the dish, and I thought I really could not possibly tell Harry that while he was out working, I had eaten half a pie. So what could I do? I ate it all.

When Harry came home, I confessed and showed him the empty pie tin, and once again, I started to cry. He just laughed, but very sweetly, and he said, "Don't worry, Barbara. We'll get another pie." And we ate our sad little dinner, which was probably a can of tuna or soup, with tears in our eyes and big smiles because we were happy to be together. Of course, there would be many more pies, but what mattered was that we could enjoy *not* having that pie as much as we would have enjoyed sharing it. If you want to know what love looks like, it looks like that.

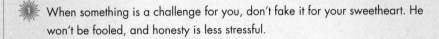

CUTIE'S COUNSEL

1. When something is a challenge for you, don't fake it for your sweetheart. He won't be fooled, and honesty is less stressful.

2. Dinnertime is about more than just sustenance; it's the part of the day when the household can be together and enjoy being a family. Plan your meals accordingly.

3. Every person has a heritage, and some lucky couples have two between them. Learn to cook a few things symbolic of your people, and it will give your children a tradition they can pass down to their kids.

4. When somebody makes her best effort and still fails, be kind. When a person is already beating herself up, if you join in, that's a mob.

THE SOCIAL WHIRL

Because my parents first made their home together in Cairo, Egypt, all I knew growing up was the Arab tradition of hospitality. This meant that we were always delighted to welcome guests, and it was our duty to make them feel almost *too* welcome.

All their favorite delicious foods would be served, the most comfortable chairs would be offered up to them, and nobody would dare suggest that it was awfully late and perhaps (yawn) we all should be getting to bed. A guest was an opportunity for everybody to enjoy the benefits of having someone special in the home. And so when Harry and I had our home together, I made certain that guests always felt welcome—though we found our own modern, California style of doing things.

Of our friends, Harry and I were among the first to have children. And because we could not afford babysitting, from the start our social activities were child-friendly. We didn't want to be without our friends just because we were parents, so we would put the children to bed and have dinner parties in the living room. If you wanted to see the Coopers, you would simply go to their house. We were always home and happy to see you. Nobody needed a formal invitation or expected a complete meal. We served food constantly—nothing elaborate, but our guests never went home hungry. With fruit platters and cookies, or cheese and bread, you can make almost anybody happy, and it's not too expensive or too much work to make a nice presentation.

Once we built our big house in Beverlywood, we had a wonderful centerpiece for entertaining: the swimming pool. Here in Los Angeles in the summer, everyone either wants a pool or to lounge by somebody else's pool. It is a whole different world when the party is poolside. For one thing, you can dress casually and not worry about your hair or your makeup. And the men are in charge of the cooking, which means a lot of meat over the fire, and the women are expected to relax. The boys enjoy behaving like cavemen, and while they express themselves in this way, the girls can go to the end of the pool away from the smoke and gossip about their husbands and neighbors and kids. The men would talk about their jobs and whatever it is men talk about.

We were never extremists. If we had people over, it did not have to be for filet mignon. But although we ran the house very simply, when there was money, more money was spent on the table. It made us happy to make our friends happy and to splurge. And when there wasn't money, nobody knew it. We were the same hosts and never complained to our friends that it was expensive to feed them.

Before too long, we found that it was helpful to have a little structure to the evening, so we began playing cards—not for high stakes, but quite passionately, all the same. The nice thing about playing cards was that it was an excuse for the men and women to sit down together. I'd put up a pot of coffee, the cookies would disappear, and the game took on a life of its own. At the end of the night, if someone had played very well, he or she might go home with sixty cents—high rollers we were not.

The couples who came were nice, like us. They mostly lived nearby and often walked to our house. Only once do I remember a couple who came and didn't fit in. They were friends of an in-law, and I found the husband a little too angry and too rough. Every other word out of his mouth was stronger than what we would have used. I was polite but glad when he and his wife did not return. I expect he found me as trying as I found him.

CHAPTER 2 :: MAKING A MARRIAGE

And so we became one of the social centers of our small community. With the passing years, this role evolved. Our kids got older, and their friends were always around the pool. Then the kids grew up and made their own homes. We settled in with our card-playing coffee klatch, and the barbecue didn't get much use. But all through our lives together, we always had people outside the family who were a big part of our lives, and we enjoyed opening up our home to good friends.

I think if you can make a home where kind people like to gather, then your marriage has brought something special into the world. Looking back, I feel proud and happy that we played this role for the families that we called our friends, and I hope that they think of us as fondly as I do them. We benefited very much from our warm relationships over the years, and I still can feel the joy of those evenings, all these years later, when I remember them.

CUTIE'S COUNSEL

 Splurge on the things that bring real pleasure to the people you love: good food, unique experiences, a comfortable space to gather in. You'll be far richer than if you rack up bills for material possessions that can't be freely shared.

If good people feel happy in your home, your marriage makes the world a better place.

FAITH

Now the fact is, neither Harry nor I was ever a very religious person. Although we considered ourselves to be Jewish, we did not grow up in observant households, and we did not feel the draw to make worshipping God a big part of our lives together.

So perhaps you will find it funny that I recommend that everyone make some room for spirituality and faith in his or her home. But I have found that a little faith goes a long way, and in hard times, you will be so grateful that you have that helping handle to hold on to.

For an irreligious person, I find it funny how often I thank God. Gratitude is a very important part of keeping a healthy attitude, and if I do not know who or what to thank, it feels easiest to thank God. And when I have nobody else to talk to, God is always happy to listen to me. I don't know if there is a God, or what kind of God exists, or where, but it makes me feel better to talk to this entity, where talking out loud to myself would only make me feel self-conscious.

I've lived a long time, and had many adventures—positive and not so positive. In my experience, most people are good, and this goodness will find its way to the surface, where it spreads. The majority of us are striving to live a righteous life, whether we are following the dictates of Jesus or Buddha or Jehovah or another deity.

If you have anything to be grateful for, then you can say thank you. If you are healthy and have a roof over your head, if you are able to enjoy the sunshine, thank God for that. Sometimes I thank God that I live in a country where I am free to believe whatever I wish to believe, and nobody will fault me for speaking my mind.

Whoever you are, whatever your circumstance, there is something you can be thankful for.

When you have some faith in your heart, then you have a wonderful oar for steering through the times when your life's waters get muddy or rough. Maybe you do not understand why things are so hard, but you know you are a good person and that you are behaving as best you can—or if you are not behaving well, you know that you ought to do so and that you will try harder. With faith and good intentions, you will not feel frightened or alone.

The times when I have been confused or brokenhearted by my situation, it has always helped me to meditate on the idea that God loves and watches over me. This is, I think, something every person wants to believe, that there is something bigger than you looking out for your well-being. We get this idea as little children, when we are allowed to explore our surroundings knowing that the big, warm animal that feeds and hugs us is somewhere close ensuring that we are not in harm's way.

And it's funny, but looking back over my life with Harry, those occasional times when we did go to temple to worship with our children and community seem like they were very important moments. I think of us in the temple, and the memory is very beautiful. I liked being part of that tradition, and I liked the recognition we felt from my parents and the other older people.

So to you I say: believe a little. It really does make life better.

1. Even if you are not religious, you may find that clinging to certain rituals gives you a peaceful feeling. Find the aspects of spirituality that speak to your needs, and let them help you in times of stress.

2. It's wise to have some spiritual outlet in your life, because with spirituality comes such positive attributes as trust, optimism, and hope. Who would want to live without them?

3. Thanks can be given to people as well as to God. Every home should have a supply of printed thank-you notes or pretty envelopes and matching paper so you can write your own. Get into the habit of thanking the people who are there for you, formally and verbally. Recognition of kindness keeps good feelings flowing long after the act has ended.

THE SPARK

A marriage is many things, some of them obvious, others elusive. It is a union of two individual lives, from possessions to dreams and all in between. It is a model to a couple's children on how they might wish to grow up and behave. It is an important building block for the community, because friends learn a lot from watching the relationships around them. And it is for many of us the most important and influential connection we will ever experience.

But to my way of thinking, the most important thing about a marriage is that it is a *passionate* thing that feeds you, body and soul. You should never get married to somebody unless the thought of that person makes you weak around the knees and fluttery in the tummy. No matter how well you get along as "friends" or how it seems like the right thing to do, unless you are passionately fascinated by the person, don't waste his or her time or yours by talking marriage—and don't be afraid to pull the plug pre–wedding bells if either one of you starts getting bored.

Anyone who saw me with Harry remarked on how often we touched one another. We were always kissing, or taking each other's hand, or just leaning our shoulders together like a pair of cats. This physicality grounded and calmed us, and whenever we reunited after being apart for a time, the first thing we did was to complete that physical circuit, and then relax. When you are with somebody, you know whether you fit into the groove or you don't. If you have to question whether he or she is the right person, then he or she is not. If you have to question if you feel a physical attraction, you don't. I believe that marriages are made in heaven, but compatibility is a very essential part to relationships—certainly it was to our relationship!

Once the vows have been exchanged, and the honeymoon is over, there's always the chance that a couple might slip into dangerous patterns that can numb the passion that brought you together in the first place. So, before you lose sight of what's really important, stock up on some lovers' tips for keeping the spark alive, and keeping yourself feeling wonderful about your marriage and yourself.

Did you know that you are beautiful—and fascinating, too? You must be, or your spouse would not have fallen so hard for you. Just because you're married now, that's no excuse to stop caring about how you look, how you carry yourself, or whether you stay well informed so you can make conversation with your sweetheart.

In fact, with divorce so common these days, you should probably work harder once you're married to remain attractive and interesting.

This is not to say that you ought to be anxious all the time while fighting a losing battle against the clock and its inevitable impact on your body. Yes, we are all getting older, but look at a silver fox like Sean Connery or an eternally elegant lady like Audrey Hepburn, and you'll see that there are ways of aging gracefully and comfortably in your skin.

Unless you have married a real rotten egg—in which case, you have my permission to get a divorce—your spouse does not want to run around behind your back and break your heart. They want what we all want: to have a happy and fulfilling relationship with the person who they fell madly in love with, and love more and more every day of their lives together. They want to be one-half of the relationship that is the envy of all their friends, to grow old hand in hand, to feel always that they were meant to be as one.

Even in the middle of the male midlife crisis that so many ladies write to me seeking help to understand and navigate, if you could sit that crisis-stricken fellow down and *really talk* with him about how he sees the rest of his life unfolding, he'd probably admit that on the other side of the immediate excitement of the new sports car or tropical vacation with that twentysomething office assistant, he doesn't have any real plans for living his life well to its end. Midlife crisis is usually just panic in the face of getting older, and it's more about the panicky person than his unfortunate rejected partner.

But if you keep your wits about you and work hard to fill your life and your marriage with what really matters, odds are good that you won't have to struggle through somebody else's months-long panic attack. And even if your foolish sweetheart does run off to try to be young again, you'll be in a much better position to move on with your life if you're already fit and happy.

Feeling good about yourself starts with feeling good inside your body. Listen to your body: it will tell you what it needs. Give it good, healthy food to eat; take it for a regular spin around the block; make sure it gets enough rest; and treat it to the little luxuries that make it feel wonderful.

For me, a bubble bath has always been just what the doctor ordered. Whether I'm stressed or tired, taking time for a soak puts the focus back on respecting and honoring myself. By the time I get out and dry off, whatever problems were troubling me are that much easier to face. Just remember not to bring your worries with you to the tub!

There is something you may like just as much as bubble baths. It is something that's not all bad for you, and it makes you always feel all right. Maybe it's putting the leash on your dog and taking a stroll through the nearest park, or slipping off to read a few chapters of your favorite novel, or turning up the music and dancing around the living room. It could be splurging on a favorite luxury edible and savoring it all by your lonesome.

Find it, and give that gift to yourself.

Feeling good is great medicine. But looking good, and knowing that you do, is just as important. It's simply a matter of self-respect. Whatever your shape, or the shape of your face, there are ways for you to bring out

the best in yourself. That means taking a critical look in the mirror and making sure that you're doing what you can to make yourself shine.

Chances are, if you work outside the home in any way that has you interacting with the public, you already make an effort to look good there. But what about when you're home with your sweetheart? Does your around-the-house uniform consist of a holey T-shirt and baggy, stained sweatpants? Toss those icky things in the trash, and let's get serious. There's no rule that says comfort and elegance cannot coexist, but I can assure you, dressing like a slob at home sends a very clear message to your spouse that you don't think he is important enough to dress for. Change that message by investing in attractive, well-fitting, comfortable loungewear.

For the fellows, it's important to get over the idea that just because you've had a piece of clothing since you were in high school, it has some magical qualities that render it forever a favored part of your wardrobe. If you're emotionally attached to some stained rag that shows your stomach when you lift up your arms, for goodness' sake, just stash it away in the back of your sock drawer and bring it out once in a while to give it an affectionate sniff. But please don't subject the person you love to the sight of you looking ragged and grubby.

For a surprisingly small sum of money each year, a gentleman can enjoy socks that match, underpants that stay up under their own steam, and casual shirts and pants that are cozy to lounge in but are still suitable for answering the door when a guest drops by unexpectedly. And his wife can enjoy looking at a nicely turned-out fellow in the comfort of their own home.

So you look good, he looks good, you like each other's looks, and you're both making an effort to stay fit. That's a wonderful way of handling the external things, but keeping the spark alive goes much deeper than that. Ideally, your partner is your best friend in the world. What do best friends do? They confide in each other, support one another's dreams, and always expend the extra effort to make life easier and more pleasant for their friend. By always striving to be a wonderful *friend* to your romantic partner, you'll find that the romance stays alive, even if there's nothing very romantic going on.

There's a special feeling you get when you realize that someone has really thought about what he or she can do to make you happy. It is a real-life manifestation of their love, and far more powerful than just saying the words "I love you" or coming home with flowers. Any stranger could say "I love you" or pick out a nice bouquet, but only the person who loves and knows and treasures you more than anybody else is going to figure out the little things that will mean the most to you, and do them as if they are the most natural things in the world. No showing off, just acting with love and thoughtfulness. It means everything.

And once in a while, you can do something very special for your sweetheart, and make a fuss about it. Like when I agreed to go up the Amazon River with Harry, at the end of a shoe-buying expedition in Buenos Aires. I do not like to rough it, and I'm scared of snakes, but this was a dream that Harry had nurtured for many years. Myself, I would have rather gone to Paris or even stayed home. But I kept thinking about how happy it would make Harry, and my mother encouraged me to go. It was my pleasure to accompany him and to see his joy, although it was not my pleasure to be up the smelly, snaky Amazon!

By giving me all his best attention, all through his life, Harry built up my ego, and it made me feel like a queen. I never had to worry if he was bored with me or our marriage, because when I saw his eyes light up, I knew our love was strong. We never played games to make the other one feel unsure or insecure. We didn't know how to play games.

We never pretended not to care as much as we cared, and anything we felt, we felt sincerely.

When we were dating, I could not imagine turning my back to Harry if he asked for a kiss and teasing, "Maybe I'll kiss you tomorrow." However, I knew girls who would say such things to their beaux. Teasing begets teasing, and I did not wish to get teased back, so such verbal play was not for me. Also, I knew that Harry thought I was pretty special, so I didn't want to disappoint him.

Only by giving love unselfishly can you receive the love you're looking for.

So if your sweetheart wants to do something, and it is a reasonable thing to want to do, support him. When Harry wanted to buy a boat, I said sure, although sailing was not my passion. I let him do what he wanted and didn't get in his way, and he did the same for me. I don't remember him wanting to do something and I said no. We found it easier to live this way.

I believe that one of the biggest threats facing couples today is overstimulation. Everyone is so busy and so distracted. I see this in the young people I know, how they can be listening to my wise remarks with one ear, but at the same time, their eyes are darting around and their fingers are reaching for their computers or telephones. I think they are addicted to information, and if they're not careful, they'll pay a price.

If you want your relationship to survive and to thrive, you will have to train yourself to focus most of your attention on the person you love. When your sweetheart comes into the room, whether it's just from taking care of some chores in the garage or from a long day at work, your job is to put down whatever you're doing, look him in the eye, and verbally express your delight at seeing him again. Don't be corny; don't be phony; just give him the benefit of your care and your affection in a way that feels real and sincere to you. It might take a few tries to get it right, but if you do, you'll soon find that it's second nature.

Have you ever played with an air-filled balloon? Do you remember how you can flick it up with the slightest bit of energy, and it will soar to the ceiling, then drop down again? Flick, soar, drop. Whatever kind of day your sweetheart is having, your smile and words of love will send him right up to the top, emotionally, and keep him coming back to get that wonderful feeling that only you can give him. It's really so little to ask, and delivers so much—to both of you.

Stress, *schmess*. There's nothing so important that your partner should be ignored when he or she comes in the door. For seventy-three years, Harry and I practiced this simple habit, and it kept us both buoyed up in good times as well as bad. I have been around the world, viewed the most exquisite buildings and famous paintings, but if you asked me to tell you about the most beautiful things on earth, I would describe my husband's smile and how his eyes crinkled up whenever he saw me come into the room.

My hope for you is that you will come to know a smile like Harry's, and that your smile will make the person you adore feel as loved as his did me.

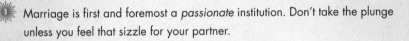

CUTIE'S COUNSEL

1. Marriage is first and foremost a *passionate* institution. Don't take the plunge unless you feel that sizzle for your partner.

2. After the wedding is no time to slack off. You worked hard to look good for your wedding guests, and you should care just as much how you look for the person you love.

3. For maximum mental health, seek out a relaxing pleasure that can be counted on to rejuvenate your soul, and don't neglect to pamper yourself regularly.

4. Pay attention. One of the most important things you can do for the good of your relationship is to never take the one you love for granted.

CHAPTER 2 :: MAKING A MARRIAGE

MAKING WHOOPEE

Each generation thinks that it invented lovemaking, but I happen to know from experience that sex has been around for a long, long time. And if you are fortunate, it will be a part of *your* experience for as long as you are alive.

The difference in my generation was that we did not talk about it. There was no sex education in the home or at school, and this wasn't a topic for conversation among my friends. I certainly cannot imagine talking about sex with my parents. There were parts of life that were private then. But somehow we still managed to find partners, have children, and enjoy ourselves in the bedroom . . . and occasionally other places, though, of course, we still did not talk about it.

Normal sex is not a talking thing. I think people who talk a lot about sex don't know anything about the subject. Don't talk about it. Just do it!

For Harry and me, sex was simply a natural extension of the fact that we wanted to be together, all the time and in every way. It is definitely the case that we got married as quickly as we did in part because we wanted to have sex, and for me that would not be happening out of wedlock.

There had been other men in my life before Harry, but dating him was the first time when I didn't feel like hugging was enough. With other dates, if I liked him, I didn't mind a little physical affection. However, there was a clear line between what felt appropriate and what was no longer comfortable.

When I was a girl, my friends played kissing games. I always sat them out. I didn't like the chance that I would have to kiss somebody I did not want to kiss. Some people look for the thrill; I look for the sincerity.

When I fell in love with Harry, I found that I felt differently about my own limits. That helped me to understand that this was really love and not the infatuation that I had felt for Ira in New York. I loved everything about Harry. I loved being in his arms and all that happened in his arms.

I just thought about Harry—I didn't connect it with sex. I connected him with me. Sex was part of it, but it was not a clinical thing in my mind. We didn't say the words that defined the acts. But when the day was done and we got into bed together, he loved me, he kissed me, and one thing led to another.

I don't understand couples who say they are too busy or too tired to sleep together. Unless they are building roads all day or running a multinational corporation, I expect they have just lost sight of priorities. If you wish to stay connected and happy in your marriage, my advice to you is to never be too tired or too busy to feel love for your partner. Even if you think you feel exhausted, relax and see what happens, and you may find you are not as pooped as you thought you were.

When your life is nearly over, you will regret it if you look back and recall too many nights when you made excuses instead of making love.

Maybe I was just very lucky in love. Harry and I were compatible. If he wanted to be more adventurous in the bedroom than I did, he didn't tell me so. And I was glad that he was more sexually experienced than I was, because I didn't know *anything*. So I learned from him, which is how we liked it. I never had to worry about him losing interest or seeking affection with someone other than with me.

But comparing our life together to the lives of people who have problems in the bedroom, I see a lot of things that we did right, without even realizing there was a way to do them wrong.

If we *had* been having a hard time in this regard, I would not have hesitated to go to a marriage counselor. There is no shame in asking for help. When you are sick, you visit the doctor. You go to the accountant to figure out your tax obligation. Good professional help is worth the cost—if you can afford the bill. Or maybe you can read a book and find helpful tools inside it. Your goal should be to have a happy, healthy life, and knowing when to ask for help is a good sign that you will make it through whatever is troubling you.

So as long as both parties are looking for solutions, I think that you will find them. There are no problems between a couple who cares about each other that cannot be solved with a little compromise and a lot of understanding and acceptance. But if one person wants to change and the other does not, please do yourself a favor and recognize that you have a bigger problem than whatever small thing you hope to change.

I am not naive. I understand that the world is different now, and a lot of young people, and older people, too, experience sex outside of marriage. Sometimes the goal is not to experience a long relationship. But even a short relationship should be based on mutual respect and leave both partners feeling good about having made the connection. Talking with my grandchildren and going to the movies has kept me up to date on how things are different from when I was a girl. People are waiting longer to get married, which is perhaps the biggest difference. Romance has not changed so very much, and my advice for those seeking love hasn't changed either.

If you would like to be intimate with another person, you should get to know him or her first. You ought to like this person a lot and feel confident that he or she will treat you with respect, kindness, and consideration. *Hoping* that this will be the case is not enough—you must wait, spend a lot of time together, and watch how this person behaves. If a prospective partner can't be bothered to behave appropriately before you are intimate, has very little time to get to know you, or does not wish to wait before enjoying intimacy, you should not be surprised when adding sex to the mix just makes matters worse.

As in so many important things, your intuition and self-respect will guide you. Ask some basic questions of yourself as you get to know this person. Do you feel comfortable with him or her? Do you enjoy this person's point of view? If you had a library book due, is this somebody you'd trust to return it?

Some unusual people appear to be *the most wonderful* potential partners, bright and thoughtful and romantic, everything you could possibly desire. But there is sometimes something strange about these delightful individuals—they seem to have no close friends or any social life except for spending time with their new favorite person: you.

Hold on a minute. Do you really think that somebody this special would have managed to live his or her entire life without making any connections before he or she encountered you? So be careful if somebody seems too good to be true. The best partners are just good enough to be true, and get better with age.

I think that the most important questions about entering into a sexual relationship can be the hardest ones to answer.

Ask yourself: What will the consequences be if I become intimate with this person?

What is the emotional and physical price I could pay?

Who do I have to answer to?

And will I feel sorry afterward?

These are not very sexy things to think about, and I am certain that they are the last questions on your mind when you are giddy with attraction and excitement, but they are real and important concepts that can protect you from being badly hurt. Please take the time to be a little bit boring and look after your own well-being before it is too late to protect yourself. Only you know which questions are most important, and which answers you can live with.

Women are more vulnerable than men in this regard. We can become pregnant. We seem to be more easily hurt when a partner betrays us. But I think that men and women want much the same thing, and my advice can help anyone who is looking to fall in love—for life or for the current season.

There's nothing wrong with the welling up of feelings that accompany new attraction. Everyone who ever fell in love with a soul mate felt that way at the start. But so did a great many people who briefly fell for some bad apple and got to experience not just the initial thrill, but also all the awful feelings that come from a bruised or broken heart.

So be careful with the butterflies in your stomach. You must learn to recognize whether you're feeling *nervous* in a good way (excited and eager) or *edgy* in a bad way (anxious and afraid). Sometimes these complicated feelings get all mixed up inside, and it can be confusing to recognize how you are feeling and why. Use your brain to protect your heart. Don't rush. Love smart now so you can love foolishly later.

So instead of just telling yourself "I like this person" and hopping up and down with excitement, try to articulate *what* you like about him. Do you mainly like his appearance and how he makes you feel, or are you truly attracted to the person inside? The things that you are able to say about him, as you get to know him, will help answer these questions.

These are the types of phrases I hope you will say as you get to know a potential new partner better: "I like how he remembered to ask how things went with my big presentation at work today." "I like how he is friendly and polite to the waitress." "I like that he has a core group of close friends who sincerely welcomed me when we met." "I like that he calls when he says he will." "I like that he has a plan for where he wants his life to go next."

If all that you can say in this person's support is "He's handsome, he's got a nice car, he spends money on me, and I like his clothes," let me remind you that you might say the exact same things about a thousand different people. Of course, you may want these things in a potential partner, but you also want more.

If you decide you will be satisfied with the superficial, please do not come crying to me should you discover all is not perfect about your "perfect" pal.

When a person is truly nice and considerate in everyday life, I think you will discover that he is equally well qualified to participate in meaningful intimate moments. Someone who respects his partner will keep the relationship wheels spinning all the time, in and out of the bedroom, and that is the type of person who will make you happy, whatever your relationship goals.

Positive attributes in an attractive partner are a bonus, but negative attributes in an attractive partner are warnings that you should not ignore. And if, as you get to know a person, you discover things about him that you hesitate to articulate to yourself, and you pretend they are not there, then you are walking on thin ice. Bad relationships thrive on secrecy. Don't keep secrets out of shame or close your eyes to things you find distressing.

If you are looking to begin a relationship that will last your whole life, you must take some risks. Nobody knows what tomorrow will bring, and although I may ask God, he does not always answer. So I think you should go out with your eyes open and try to find someone worth loving. If it doesn't work out, I hope it doesn't work out with someone who is kind and leaves you with good memories. There is a partner for every person. If you put the same thought and energy into finding that partner as you do picking a job, a school, what color dress to buy, or where you will live, you have a good chance of picking wisely.

In my experience—which has been limited but very happy—there is wonderful sex to be had in a committed relationship based on mutual attraction, respect, and shared values. We do not always advertise the fact, but squares like me really know how to have a good time.

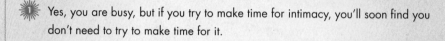
1. Yes, you are busy, but if you try to make time for intimacy, you'll soon find you don't need to try to make time for it.

2. Treat a relationship with the same care and skepticism that you apply to making a major purchase or life choice. It's fine to feel excited, but don't be so excited that you stumble into something that will make you miserable.

THE JOY OF DRIVING EACH OTHER NUTS

In fairy tales, after much storm and stress, Prince Charming finally finds his princess, and the two of them gallop off to the castle together for what we are given to understand will be a life packed to the rafters with absolutely everything *except* petty annoyances and irritations.

I can assure you, even royal couples get on each other's nerves, and so did Harry and I.

You will, too. It's perfectly normal.

Anytime two people come together to share a home and a life, they might as well just resign themselves that there will be times when they are ready to scream, tear their hair out by the roots, and run down the castle driveway in their pajamas.

Now whether you actually behave like this depends on how high-strung you are and how comfortable you are with the thought of the earl across the way seeing you in your nightclothes. But these feelings are inevitable. Healthy people recognize the challenges that living together introduce to their lives, and they develop skills for coping with them.

Don't make the romantic mistake of thinking it all has to be perfect all the time, and if it's not, you'll just pretend. Irritations are amazing. They start out like an itch, turn into an ache, and if you let them fester long enough, they can really hurt you and your relationship. But if you make an effort to notice what bothers you, and encourage your partner to do the same, then you'll have the invaluable opportunity to talk your troubles out before they get to the painful stage. The euphemism is "letting off steam," or "venting." Well, think about it. If you don't let the steam off, you're going to have a messy blowup. Personally, I'd rather open my mouth up and let that steam out before I don't have a choice about it.

I think that there are very few conflicts that can't be made better simply by talking it out. But it is very important that you not mistake this process for one in which at the end of the conversation, the losing person must bend to the winning person's needs. It's often enough that he tells you his side, you tell him where you don't agree, and then you can agree to disagree.

There is an old Jewish saying that if you put two Jews together, they will have three opinions. I think it's okay if I have different ideas than the person I love. We don't need 100 percent agreement to love each other or to go on living. Actually, I think I would be bored with a partner who had no differences in his opinions. Listen—love is important, but love is nothing without acceptance.

Certainly with big issues, like how to raise children or where to live, you will need to pick one way of doing things as a family and both stick to it. But there are smaller conflicts that can be worked out simply through communication and mutual respect, where no one person needs to come out on top. Learn to recognize problems that require complete cooperation, and those that don't, and you'll be one step closer to happiness.

Harry was not perfect, and neither was I. But we always believed that we were perfect for each other, and so we cut one another plenty of slack. I never expected Harry to be something that he wasn't, and he was tolerant of me with all my—well, let's call them *idiosyncrasies* rather than *flaws,* since that's a much nicer way of putting it, and closer to how Harry saw my quirks.

Acceptance is the gift I tried to give my children, and it is the great secret to getting along with people. You cannot change a person, but you can understand and support and love him—and if you do that, perhaps he will not mind changing the little things that you don't like so much, or at least he will go off to practice them in private.

One thing that Harry and I always held on to was our senses of humor, and a sense of humor is something I recommend you develop if you're not fortunate enough to have one already.

What's the big deal about a sense of humor? I really believe it was the grease that kept our relationship cranking along for seventy-three years. There's an old saying, probably Jewish, that laughter is the best medicine. It's wonderful stuff, laughter. It kind of helps the day go by and helps you face reality—even if reality's face isn't so pretty at the moment. Being able to laugh at our troubles always helped Harry and me to muddle through.

Not everyone is naturally funny, but nearly everybody has a sense of humor and can improve it. Do so; you will not regret it!

Being able to give things a humorous spin permits you to obtain a different perspective, so everything isn't so dire and somber. Gallows humor is probably the most valuable kind, since if you can't laugh when things are really falling down around you, all you can do *is* cry. But having the sensitivity to know how to turn a bit of tragedy into comedy in a way that is not offensive, but that helps the people around you who are suffering—that's the great power of humor. Because the wailing and the crying and the beating your breast do not really solve your problem, but a little laughter goes a long way toward starting the healing process.

If you should have a choice of whether to laugh or to cry, laugh. Laughing makes you stronger, and it does not diminish the seriousness of a situation. I think instead of turning an already bad situation into a tragedy, make it into a comic strip.

One very important use of humor is turning it on yourself when you get so mad at something your spouse has done, said, or failed to do or say that you feel like you are about to blast off through the roof and go into orbit. That's an excellent moment to get outside of yourself, recognize how ridiculous you are, and, through laughter, defuse the bomb inside you.

That kind of anger is extremely dangerous. Have you ever noticed that you can't spell *dangerous* without *anger*? I'm no linguist, but I don't think that's a coincidence. When you're ready to blow, you might say anything hurtful, things you would normally spare the person you love from hearing. Don't say something you'll regret forever. Don't give your partner an excuse to come back to you with his or her own resentments.

Instead, find a way to get your anger under control. I do get angry, but I don't hold on to it for long. For myself, I simply run through my mind a short movie of how foolishly I have been acting, and then I say to myself, quite firmly, "Barbara, stop being so foolish! Turn the page and face the new day." That works for me, because I am like a mistress telling the part of myself who is a bad dog to behave. You may have better luck singing a silly song, or patting your head while rubbing your tummy, or doing whatever little trick helps bring you outside of yourself long enough to regain control.

And never hold a grudge. If you're mad about something, find a healthy way to get it out into the open and resolve it, and then don't bring it up again the next time that you're mad. For a relationship to grow, you need to keep moving and not stake yourself down to past disagreements.

Up until I married, I had not seen a great many relationships. My parents seemed very contented to me, although my father was definitely the squeaky wheel in our home. When I was older, my mother confided that things were not actually perfect between them. I am glad that whatever issues they had, my father's conduct in the home was always respectful toward his bride, and I learned to expect the same from my husband.

I think Harry was a nicer person than I am. Nothing got under his skin, and he always supported me in my aspirations. If somebody was driving me crazy, he would say, "Well, Barbara, there are people and people and people," by which he meant some folks were simply impossible, and what could you do? So a lot of the success in our marriage must be credited to him. He was easy to love and easy to live with. If I hadn't found Harry, I might not have all this good advice to share with you.

I'm not naive. I know that relationships are hard and that many couples fail to find a way to live happily and productively together. My feeling is that if you're going to take the risk of beginning a serious relationship with another person, you may as well put in the effort it takes to find the best way to get along with your partner. Every person is different, but every reasonable person can be reached—if you go about it the proper way for the individual. Now, if you have decided to make your life with an *unreasonable* person, there is not a lot of advice that I can give you. Maybe you can give me some advice.

That's the best I have to offer. I think some of my theories are basic and that I am really kind of a square. But these methods have worked for me, and it is my hope that they will help you. And after seventy-three years together, or however many you get to enjoy, you can write a book, too.

CUTIE'S COUNSEL

1. It's okay to be annoyed by things that the person you love does, but it's not okay to hold grudges. If you learn to articulate the things that bother you, and be willing to bend, your partner will do the same.

2. You can think something completely differently than your sweetheart does, and you can both be right. Pick your battles, and respect your differences.

3. A sense of humor is the secret sauce that softens aggravation. Keep a pot of humor bubbling on your internal stove, and use it regularly to improve your mood and the moods of those around you.

Chapter 3: YOU ARE WHAT YOU DO

WORKING FOR OURSELVES

Should you happen to watch the popular television shows from when I was a young wife and mother, programs like *The Donna Reed Show* and *Father Knows Best,* you would be forgiven for thinking that all middle-class American moms stayed at home to manage their households and children.

Of course, such was the experience of many women of my acquaintance, and for some families, this was a fine way to exist. But it was not right for the Coopers. For the first few years of our marriage I did stay home and did the best I could to cook and clean and coordinate. Our daughter Carol was the thoughtful one, and our son Jan was a charmer who wanted to be wherever the people were. As long as the children were small, I was in the home to care for them, and as I recall, we had a great deal of fun.

But as my children grew and started school, the house seemed very confining. I was bored on my own, and I missed Harry. And Harry felt hemmed in working for somebody else. We lived in Los Angeles, which was a growing city with many opportunities for young people willing to use their brains and their backs to make their way in life. When I think back on the early years of our marriage, I am amazed at all the different things that Harry—and later I—did to make a living.

When we wed, Harry had a pretty good job driving a truck delivering gourmet Swedish foods around the city. I suppose this is where he developed his sophisticated palate and habit for eating weird things that nobody else in the family would even consider putting in their mouths (although I did enjoy the lingonberry preserves).

Every morning, he got into his truck, picked up his deliveries, and carried these goodies to the small markets and delicatessens where these items were sold. He lugged huge vats of potato salad to the Grand Central Market, and pickles to Philippe the Original, and along the way he developed some very attractive muscles and learned all the secret shortcuts of Los Angeles. Part of his job was developing new customers, and his good looks, sweet personality, and genuine fondness for what he was selling made him very good at his job.

But you can't make much money working for somebody else, and with a family to support, Harry decided it was time to go out on his own. I said, "Great! Let's find something you can do where I can help!"

Harry knew the wholesale food business moderately well, and he got a lead on a shop in Long Beach that sold live chickens. In Los Angeles in the 1940s, roadside chicken restaurants were big business—that's how the famous Knott's Berry Farm got started. And all of those restaurants needed to get their chickens somewhere, so why not from us? We agreed to purchase this operation from the funny little old guy who had started it, so we squeezed into his truck to tour everything that made the business function.

It just goes to show that you can't make any presumptions about another person. This little man ran a successful store with a lot of moving parts, but he could neither read nor write. When we first drove out to the farm where we were to purchase each day's chickens—after determining what price to pay per pound by listening to the radio farm report before dawn—this man didn't know the name of a single road or business. He simply told us, "You'll turn right when you get to the big oak tree next to the oil well" and "Look out for the lima-bean field, and then you'll know you're almost there." Well, we found the farm, stocked up on birds, and hung up our shingle. Harry rigged up a funny little moving chicken sign that made folks interested enough to stick their heads inside and see what we were all about.

Our business was in providing fresh chickens to restaurants and individuals. Our birds were so fresh that they were alive and clucking when you bought them but dead and ready for the stew pot when you left our shop.

Did I mention that I cannot stand chickens? I don't like to eat them, and I didn't much like spending my day in their company, and there was no way on God's green earth that you would catch me wringing a chicken's neck. So my job in the store was manning the counter and interacting with customers, while Harry—or sometimes the rabbi, if we were making a kosher preparation—would do the dirty work of killing and cleaning these unfortunate creatures.

Business was good, but I was not happy. The chickens made me nervous while they were alive and sad when they were dead. And mostly, I missed my family. There were no freeways in those days, so it was a big deal to drive all the way up to Los Angeles for a visit. Long Beach was pretty sleepy, except when the fleet was in town, when it got rowdy. And so before too long, we let the chicken business go and moved back to the big city.

It was around this time that the troubles in Europe got too bad to ignore. We were fortunate that most of our family members were safe in the United States or South America—I just had one uncle left in France, and he made it through in one piece and married a Catholic lady, who he adored.

When the war broke out, Harry didn't have to worry about being drafted, because he had already served in the peacetime army as a young man. However, this did not mean that we were not separated. One thing about my Harry, if he had to work for a living, he would always find the job that paid the best. During the war, the best-paying jobs were in the shipyards, and that sometimes meant long weeks apart while he lived where the work was.

Maybe you have heard of a boilermaker—which is a job, not just a drink—but have you ever heard of a boilermaker's assistant? Because Harry didn't have a background in factory work, this was as high as he rose in the shipyard trade.

His job was to follow along behind the boilermaker, who was welding huge pieces of steel together, and to provide this man with a regular supply of fresh, red-hot rivets (or, as Harry insisted on pronouncing them, "ribbets"). There was another fellow nearby, heating the rivets over a hot fire and throwing them at my Harry. So he had to be constantly looking out for hot bits of steel flying his way, catching them in a bucket, grabbing them with tongs, and plopping them into the holes a few inches away from the boilermaker's face.

These men worked hard, and it was dangerous, physical labor. I worried a lot, and I missed Harry. One time, he was in Las Vegas working on a bridge. I decided on the spur of the moment to ask my father to drive me on the desert road for a visit. Nobody had a phone then, so we just hopped into the car and set out on the long, dusty trip.

Well, somewhere along that road, we must have passed Harry, who had the same idea and was on his way to Los Angeles to see me. What could we do but laugh?

When the war ended, those steelworking opportunities went away. We talked about opening another shop together, and I made it clear that there weren't going to be more chickens in my future.

Now, as it happens, my father had gone into the shoe business, so with my parents' encouragement, Harry's skill as a low-pressure salesman (the best kind), and my passion for footwear, we decided to give that trade a try. My father, of course, had a great deal to tell us, some of it very good advice, some of it quite long-winded. We just wanted to spread our wings and make a go of things on our own, and often in the early years, my father's paternal concern could be overbearing. We learned to smile and say, "Thank you very much"—quite convincingly, I think.

Harry was an independent guy, and he was not interested in being in business with my family. Sometimes we'd go in together on a large purchase that would be shared between both stores—my father's and ours—but we were always our own bosses, and we loved it. I think we

CHAPTER 3 :: YOU ARE WHAT YOU DO

even enjoyed making mistakes, because they were our mistakes. It felt good to make it on our own.

Our shop's specialty was very nice shoes for men, women, and children that just happened to be last year's styles, which meant they were much more affordable. Unless you were a movie star, what difference did it make if your shoes were not hot off the presses? After all, when you love a pair of shoes, you'll keep wearing them for years.

Both Harry and I worked in the store and waited on customers, but I was the one who looked at all the wholesale samples and chose the very cutest styles, while Harry did the physical work, like building the shelves, polishing the stock, and separating the shoes by colors for display. And he worked longer hours when I needed to be with the children after school.

If you are thinking of going into business, especially in retail, don't kid yourself: it's a big responsibility. You should expect to be available twenty-six out of twenty-four hours—at least it feels that way. A business has to open on time and close on time. Your books and your cash register have to balance. Your responsibility to the public is to be ethical, courteous, honest, and aware of their needs. And you can't just hire a different person to do every little task; you have to become something of an expert at everything. Between us, we were the janitor, the supervisor, the stock man, the cashier, and the sales staff. And this was not a nine-to-five job; it was every night, and weekends, because we needed to be there when people were free to go shopping. Our family knew: the store came first. Retail is not for lazy people or for sloppy ones, but if you're sharp, you can make a nice living.

People like to make fun of shoe salesmen, but it was interesting work. We had to use our brains, anticipating what sizes and styles and colors our customers would want while staying within our budget. Throughout the year, we would get visits from salesmen showing what they had on offer, and once a year we'd go to the big shoe convention in downtown Los Angeles.

There were times when we'd make the wrong choice and end up with too much of a shoe that wouldn't move—then, eventually, we'd let them go to the guys whose business was dealing in twice-wholesaled product. Of course, if something really special was available in a size 4½, I didn't worry so much about the cost, since that was *my* size! I had a beautiful shoe collection, in all the *almost*-latest styles.

Years later, after we let the business go, it turned out that some very old shoes we'd stocked away at the top of the shelf had become so old that they were collectibles. If you've ever seen the movie *Grease,* those are my saddle shoes on all those happy teenagers!

And although it can be frustrating to deal with the public, we found that most customers were happy to be getting new shoes, and a bargain. For a woman, even if she's not happy with her shape, she can get a new pair of shoes, and they will always fit and give her a lift. Men are easy; they know what they like and don't want to spend much time shopping. Whole families came in together, and the kids had to be fitted, which meant they had to be encouraged to sit still in one place long enough that you could fit them. Meanwhile, someone had to stop their siblings from running up and down the aisles. I quickly learned that the most important thing any shoe store can have in stock is lollipops. The most ill-behaved child can be bribed with the promise of a sucker.

It's like any other business when you deal with walk-in customers. There are those who are a pleasure to wait on, and there are those who you are glad they came in and then *really* glad when they leave.

Our customers were savvy. They knew what they were doing when they walked in the door. If they wanted to spend a lot, they could go to the department store. Instead, they came to us, happy to walk out in a pair of sixty-five-dollar shoes for twenty-four dollars or even eighteen dollars. That was a very good markdown of a luxury item. More common would be twenty-four dollars and ninety-five cents retail and eighteen dollars and ninety-five cents from us. There had to be a good price for the public and enough left over so that you could make a living, too. Some customers would come in repeatedly, looking for something they'd admired at the

CHAPTER 3 :: YOU ARE WHAT YOU DO

department store and that was still being sold there. We tried to make them happy by carrying the best lines and getting fashionable stock in quickly.

My philosophy of working in retail is that you get what you put into it. If you start the day feeling crabby, you are sure to rub your customers the wrong way, and they're bound to give you something new to complain about. So I aimed to please. I pleased the public, and they pleased me. I never spoke down to my customers. I treated them with respect and was grateful that they picked our store out of all the options. I made an effort to sell them what they really wanted, not the stock I was in a hurry to get rid of. And I watched my language, not using words that might be offensive, because you never know who your words might fall on. I tried to be agreeable, and I usually found that a smile and a sincere exchange of words had a positive effect. I don't mean that everybody was pleasant, but the majority were.

So, that was our business, and we kept at it until we retired, around the time our first grandchild was born. What a pleasure it was, to find a way that we could share our lives all day long. Some couples are not suited to being together all the time, but for Harry and me, it always stung to separate, even for a few hours. So our little shoe store was our daytime home, and we thought of our customers as our guests. And we were happy when guests came over, though it always was fun, on rainy days when nobody wanted to buy shoes, to just hide in the back together and cuddle. And although the cash register was empty, those were the times when we thought that we really had it made.

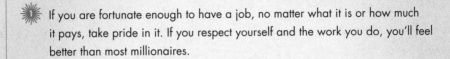

CUTIE'S COUNSEL

☀ If you are fortunate enough to have a job, no matter what it is or how much it pays, take pride in it. If you respect yourself and the work you do, you'll feel better than most millionaires.

☀ Work should not be approached as an imposition to suffer through but as a privilege. Your work is a big part of who you are, not something to endure. Come to it with a positive attitude, and all good things will follow.

☀ Work is important, and your relationships are, too. Don't put one in front of the other. Integrate and balance the significant parts of your life instead.

HIS, HERS, AND OURS

When you first fall in love with somebody, you want to spend every spare moment with that person. It feels as if you have spent your whole life searching for him or her, and now that you're together, all you want to do is to be close and learn everything there is to know about the other person.

And then one day, you wake up and you think it wouldn't be the end of the world if you had a little breathing room. You miss your girlfriends or the hobbies that are of no interest to your sweetheart, and you miss that breathless feeling of missing the person that you love.

Don't make the mistake of thinking this means you're falling out of love. Infatuation fades, and with it the emotional need for intense, constant togetherness, but in a healthy relationship, this is simply a new phase that can be even more fulfilling than that first one.

As close as Harry and I were, we both treasured our time apart. Harry and I always had our separate identities, and we enjoyed the experience of being apart because we could then come back together and catch up on what was new. Besides, all people are different, and it would be silly to think that they enjoy all the same things. There are *boy* things and *girl* things, *he* things and *me* things, and what one person finds scintillating, another might find dishwater dull. I did not expect him to like my hobbies, but I did expect Harry to give me the space to enjoy them—just as I gave him the space to enjoy his.

So recognize and respect the differences, and do not neglect the time that belongs to you, when you feed your soul. This recharging doesn't need to cost money, and you don't even need to leave the house. With me, hopping into the bathtub was always the perfect "me time." Some people bathe for two minutes. I like staying for a half hour at the minimum. This wasn't just a married lady's escape—even when I was little, my mother used to say, "Get out of the tub; somebody else wants to be clean!" I love resting in the warm water with a book in my hands and a waterproof pillow under my neck. Reading is a private thing—nobody else is interested in what you want to read. With a story to take me away, I relaxed like nobody's business, and the minutes and my tension just melted away.

Sometimes I would go out with the girls and shop or play golf. Or if I felt the need to be solitary, those could be alone activities, too. And groups of us would participate in organizations, like hosting City of Hope charity sales or making phone calls for a political cause we shared. When we were together for "girl time," we'd talk of babies and girdles and recipes and all the things the men would prefer not to know about. We were grateful for our time together, because women like to talk about their lives without worrying that the men are bored or uncomfortable.

When you have girlfriends, it's nice if your husband likes them. It can be a source of conflict when one-half of a couple is spending time with people that the partner doesn't trust or enjoy. But, happily, Harry liked my girlfriends, and these same ladies would come to our home with their husbands for dinner parties and card games.

For a little while, my girlfriend Faye and I tried to run an interior-decorating business. Really, it was a hobby, and although we didn't make a bunch of money, we had fun. Harry thought it was great, because I wanted to do it. It didn't take away from him; it added to me.

When we started the decorating business, we were what you might call suburban matrons with time on our hands. Our children were in school, and our husbands were in business. The shoe store was doing well

CHAPTER 3 :: YOU ARE WHAT YOU DO

enough that we could hire people to do much of the busywork that used to be my job. I took this as an opportunity to spread my wings.

Faye and I thought that if we got a resale license, we could visit the antique and furniture shops in Hollywood, purchase things at a discount, and sell them to our clients at a premium. And if we should happen to see something that we would like for our own homes, well . . .

We didn't go to school to be decorators. We read the decorating magazines, visited the stores, talked about what we liked and didn't like, and went from there.

The best part of being a decorator is the buying. Selling is something else again. That's the biggest mistake people make when they go into business, thinking it will be easy to sell what they have accumulated, just because they liked it. It's hard work to build a clientele; then, even when you have people willing to hire you, you must get them to write a check—and the check must not bounce!

To build the business, first we had to decorate my house and her house, because we would be bringing our potential clients—or more often our friends—in to talk about their needs. If you are supposed to be a decorator, your home had better look nice. "Oh, isn't that pretty?" "Why thank you. You know, I decorated this room myself."

And then the most important words: "I can get it for you wholesale." You always have a friend who needs something, a new lamp or a couch, although it is awkward to charge as much on top of the wholesale price as you should for your friends. But we didn't expect to rely on our income. This was mainly for fun, and it kept us out of trouble.

When you work with friends, you learn things about them that you might not have noticed previously. We didn't have any big revelations, but I certainly discovered that I was more business-oriented than Faye was. Her husband was in the clothing-manufacturing business, so she had not worked in retail like I had. I was the one who understood accounting, and display, and the basics of dealing with customers. Yes, all that sexy stuff that people fight over.

Faye didn't object if I did more of the work, but had we been successful, eventually I might have minded. You want to share the grunt work equally when you're partners. However, since we didn't have many clients, this was not a big source of conflict.

Eventually, we wound down the business and split up the stock. Although we did not become rich or famous from our efforts, our friendship survived, and so I would call this experiment in independence a true success.

Friendships outside of your marriage can be wonderfully fulfilling, but they can be a challenge, too. Recently, a Facebook friend asked how I would handle a friendship with someone who had become extremely negative. My advice was to let the friend know that you are available if he or she wishes to talk but to make a point not to get sucked into the negativity. You can't help someone who is blue by sinking to his or her level, and you may hurt yourself in the process. In my opinion, negativity will never solve your problems, so I try to err on the side of happiness instead. Even if I look silly singing that "everything's coming up roses," I like the way it makes me feel.

As for Harry, he was an outdoorsman. Any excuse to get out in the sun and move his body was one he'd take. Golf was his sport, as was tennis, when he could find a partner. He loved fishing, and I didn't mind—as long as he didn't make me go fishing or make me eat a fish. Eventually, we got a boat so he could visit the fish whenever he liked, and sailing was a passion he shared with our son, Jan.

Harry's at-home private time was usually spent in the garage, where he had his workshop. He could listen to his favorite Hawaiian records without annoying me; tackle something on my honey-do list ("Honey, do this; Honey, do that"); or putter away at one of his experiments. At one time, he was very interested in making models—models of ships, models of houses. Let me tell you, I did not want to watch him hammer a bunch of nails or glue two pieces of wood. If that is what he got a kick out of, who was I to judge?

103

Hours would pass, and he would come inside at mealtime in a wonderful mood—but then, a wonderful mood describes Harry's disposition pretty much no matter what he had been doing all day. That was the difference between us. I needed my private time to calm down from the stresses of our life, but stress did not seem to get to Harry. Lucky guy.

I was glad that we both could enjoy private times in the home, without constantly getting into each other's business. It's nice when you're both at home. I enjoyed my retreats in the bath, but I liked hearing his hammer and nails behind the closed garage door, and I guess he liked to hear me splashing in the tub. Some people need to be really alone to recharge, and others just appreciate a little bit of space.

Well, now Harry is gone, and I have a lot of alone time. And I don't like that he is gone. But it's funny—I still feel as if he is just on the other side of the garage door—even though at this stage of my life, I do not even *have* a garage. I know he is in the other world and not with me, but I can picture him at his workbench, nodding his head to his favorite Hawaiian record, puttering away. He is always nearby if I need him, and I am nearby if he needs me. And I realize that even our "me time" was always "us time," because we were together in our thoughts. We didn't have to talk or touch or see each other to feel united, and now I no longer know how to feel as if I were alone.

FALL IN LOVE FOR LIFE

CUTIE'S COUNSEL

1. If you want to stay sane and grounded, make certain that among all your other obligations, you schedule a little "me time" in your day—even if it's just a few moments behind a locked bathroom door.

2. Harry's garage was his domain, and it really mattered to him. Knowing that the man I loved could go into his private space and come out feeling wonderful made me love that dirty old garage. If you truly care for someone, you'll love the things that he loves.

3. Togetherness is great, but don't drag your partner along to an event you like and he hates. Neither one of you will be happy. Trust each other enough to allow for independent time apart, and you can both pursue your passions, then meet in the middle to catch up.

SURVIVING HARD TIMES

Wouldn't it be wonderful if every business venture that you put your hand to was a fabulous success, fulfilled you emotionally, and stuffed your bank account with lots and lots of money?

Although I wish such success to you, it's simply not possible that every person should be a King Midas at every moment. Even smart people fail, and good ideas don't always come along at the right time. Sometimes, you might even have a bad idea and be fooling yourself that it is brilliant.

And the fact is that hard work feels just as tiring when you're trying to keep a sinking ship afloat as when you're steering that gold-medal yacht through the winner's tape.

You cannot change the world, but you can always change yourself. So in the event that you should one day find that your career or business is (temporarily, of course) on the skids, you must be sure that you already have the right attitude to survive and to thrive through this or any other economic challenge.

The most important piece of advice that I can give to a person so that he or she can survive hard times is to learn to live within your means *before* the hard times hit. This is a cliché that you have heard before, so I will be more specific: figure out which luxuries in your life are *really* feeding your soul, and which ones are just clutter, habit, or laziness. You may be surprised to find out that you are making emotional spending decisions that aren't very satisfying, and there are not-so-costly things you'd really enjoy having in your life that you have completely overlooked. In our family, we never lived high. Our needs were very simple, so we were never disappointed. Whatever else, we always made sure there was money for plenty of good, nourishing food on the table—because nothing is more important than your family knowing that they will be well fed in their home.

We did not overdo it. We made do with what we had. And if circumstances were such early in our marriage that we didn't have money for meat, I simply cooked a special meatless casserole that my husband loved, lit a few candles, and made it seem like a special occasion. Attitude is everything.

When Harry and I got married, we had very little money, so our expectations were not so grand. Should we have waited to be together until we were more established? We never even considered waiting. All we wanted was to be together, and not so we could begin to live more extravagantly than we were used to.

We were young; we were in love; we made a go of life. It wasn't easy, but it wasn't hard. We didn't look for trouble. We just saw where we were along our path, where we wanted to be, and we set out together, eyes forward, hand in hand.

We didn't want more than we had, so we were satisfied. You can be satisfied, too. You can always make do. A lot of people have done so all throughout history. It's not so exciting to live within your means, but I think it's a little *too* exciting to live beyond them. My suggestions are mainly about the things that we didn't do. Don't pay more rent than you can afford. Try not to get involved with owing people money, and if you must, pay it off as soon as you are able. Don't look at how other people live and let that influence how you feel about your own experience. What makes you happy, that's all that counts.

Before our wedding, Harry bought me a simple ring, and I never wanted a bigger one. Why would I, when this ring was the one he'd used to marry me?

CHAPTER 3 :: YOU ARE WHAT YOU DO

It seems so obvious that two really can live as cheaply as one, maybe more cheaply. You do not need a whole loaf of bread; two people can share a loaf, and it will still probably get moldy before one of you reaches the heel. Who needs a three-bedroom apartment when you can sleep together in one bed? When Harry was making twenty-seven dollars a week, that's what I budgeted for, not for the thirty dollars I might have wished he was bringing home. Whatever money Harry made, that was enough for me. Twenty-seven dollars was twenty-seven dollars. I know it sounds like nothing to you, but to us, it wasn't anything to sneeze at. We had a good time on twenty-seven dollars, but we always put something away for times of need.

We knew we would have to pay the doctor when we had our children, so the way we saved was that every silver dollar that came into the house was hidden away until the day the child was born. They used to make you pay cash. I expect they would have let us leave with the baby if we hadn't had the money, but we didn't want to take that chance!

Harry let me be in charge of the household budget, which was good, because it can be confusing if both parties are in charge. I don't think I was stingy, although I did take my responsibility seriously. It seems hard to keep a budget, but it's just math. Write the numbers down, and go over them together until they aren't so intimidating.

Look, you might be reading about my life and thinking that I am a real Pollyanna who doesn't understand anything about today's finances. Well, even though we didn't have computers or credit cards when I was a young woman, we had all the same problems and worries that you have today. And just like now, some families figured out how to get along without conflict, and others struggled. Harry and I found ways to make our economic life flow along like a gentle green stream, and our methods can still help you today.

The most important ingredient for getting through difficult economic times is *THE TRUTH*—it's so important that it should be capitalized, italicized, *and* underlined. When you can talk honestly about your spending, and that of your partner, as well as what spending is done on behalf of your children, you are taking important steps toward weaving the financial safety net that all families must create in good times, so that in the event of bad ones, their home and health will be protected. So this means that if you have any financial secrets you are keeping from your partner, you must put them on the table. Doesn't that sound scary? If you are one of those secret-keepers, I am sure that it does, but as with so many unpleasant things that only get bigger and stronger in the dark, these secrets have a funny way of shrinking in the light of truth. And as they get smaller, your stress and worry will fly away.

Maybe there is a student loan you've been ignoring or a department store bill you hide each month. If so, there's never been a better time to be honest with your partner and yourself and make a plan for dealing with your debts and your excess spending—together. I promise, you will not regret it.

Because Harry and I began our life together during the Depression, we never had to learn how to keep our spending under control. If anything, we had to teach one another that it was acceptable to splurge and treat ourselves once we could afford to do so.

And although we mostly had good luck—or, in Harry's words, "the Cooper Luck"—in our business dealings, there certainly were some times when we were skating on thin ice, and we knew it. I would be lying if I told you that this was not stressful. Nobody can see into the future, so when times were hard, there was always the fear that they would stay hard or possibly get worse. We lived through several national economic scares and other dips that were limited to our household alone.

Through every one of these nerve-racking experiences, we did one very important thing that ensured we would come through it all in one piece: we never, not for one instant, took our fear and frustration out on one another.

If I made a miscalculation when deciding what styles and sizes of shoes to purchase and we ended up with worthless stock crowding our shelves, Harry just smiled and said, "You win some and you lose some. Barbara, you just have better taste than our customers sometimes, that's all." Knowing that I would not be criticized for failing, I felt confident to go out and do my best, and I did so.

And if Harry happened to hire a clean-cut kid whose idea of learning the ropes included emptying out the till and not returning to the store the following day, I would simply soothe my sweetheart's mind and point out how sad it was that some people had so little that they had to steal from folks who had a little more.

There are times when your judgment about another person may be incorrect, but I don't think that means you ought to stop trusting. Most people are good, and as long as you are not foolishly trusting, you can assume the best about others and not be too disappointed.

As for mistakes, make them all. They help you grow together. People make mistakes, and sometimes those mistakes cost money. So what? It's not like anyone sets out to make a mistake. As long as your intentions are good, you are reasonably careful, and you don't keep making the same mistakes repeatedly, I think that every person deserves to be cut a little slack—and then some more slack if a little was not sufficient.

Forgiveness is underrated, as well as very good for your relationship. In seventy-three years of marriage, I cannot think of a single thing that either Harry or I did that was worth holding a grudge over, which either means we were both absolutely perfect—which I promise you we were not—or that we had a healthy attitude about expectations and one another.

When we were having hard times, we endured them. That's the way we grew up, and I guess that we didn't know any better. We certainly didn't say, "Hmm, this is hard—I think I will give up on my marriage, since that will make everything so much easier." We didn't do a lot of talking in rough times; we just put our heads down, worked a little faster, and hoped for the sun to come up the next day. It usually did.

I used to tell my kids, "It is just as easy to fall in love with a rich person as with a poor one." But once you fall in love, you should love that person for who he or she is, as he or she should love you for who you are. The vows you make when you marry are sacred obligations, not just pretty words to pick and choose from when life gets hard.

When you are struggling, it's your choice how the struggle affects you, and it's up to you if you are going to let hard times bring you down. If you don't have much money and you still have your health, be happy that you've got your health. And if you don't have much money and you're not feeling so good, be grateful that you've still got your sense of humor. And if you don't have a sense of humor, go out and find one!

A sense of humor is not optional. Laughter has been the soundtrack of my whole life, and there is nothing that has helped more in times of worry than laughing at myself and at my circumstances. I firmly believe that there is no trouble so big that it defies laughter and no worry so severe that you cannot see its funny side. Maybe you will think I am a foolish ninny, but this little ninny has faced down some very tough times, with a smile on her face and always a sense of hope in her heart. So I suggest you not knock the ninnies!

CUTIE'S COUNSEL

1. If money is a source of worry, take an honest inventory of your spending and income. Then start over from scratch. The cold, hard truth will tell you what you need to change.

2. If you live within your means when you don't need to, tough times won't seem so tough to you.

3. If you're broke, so what? Use your imagination to live like a king or a queen. Without an imagination and a positive attitude, you are very poor indeed. With both, there are no limits to the possibilities.

TRAPEZE ACTS

I'm not going to lie to you. Work is stressful, and career issues can be one of the biggest strains on any marriage. When two people come together to make a family, they bring with them their individual skills, backgrounds, and ambitions, and you'd be foolish to think those varying things would just seamlessly mesh without effort.

In some families, two people on the career path meet, but only one person continues along that chosen route, while the other—often, but not always, the woman—becomes a homemaker and supporter of the spouse and any children the two have. In other families, both parties make allowances and sacrifices so that neither person has to give up his or her professional dreams. Then there are the families like mine, who make a new business together.

Any way you slice it, integrating home and career is hard work. But there are some tricks you can use to help your family blend these obligations with style and grace. The secret is in how you look after one another, understand your individual needs, and make sure you both talk honestly about what really matters to you.

I think it's important that both halves of a pair have the chance to do the work that calls to them, and that one of the responsibilities of a good spouse is to support your sweetheart while he or she reaches for the stars—wherever these stars happen to be located.

In our family, without being too ambitious, Harry always knew what he wanted out of his professional life. Without an education, he understood that he was limited in what he could achieve. He was not afraid of hard work, but if he was going to put his all in, he wanted to get a good wage and to be treated with respect. As we settled in to our marriage, it wasn't sufficient any longer for him to hold down a job where someone else called the shots. My Harry was not the type of person who could be content to simply be a drone in somebody else's beehive. So although I knew that he could make a good living with less risk, stress, or responsibility working for a boss, I didn't argue when he suggested going into business for himself. Instead, I put my brain to work figuring out what he could do to make this dream come true—and later, I put on my coveralls and toiled alongside him, so that we could succeed together.

We didn't want so much. A good middle-class home for our children, food on the table, a nice car to drive, money in the bank. We wanted to be able to send our children to school. We had all that. It made me proud that we didn't have to borrow or ask my family for help. We did a little better with each passing year, and it was satisfying to know that we could make it by our wits and our sweat.

It's funny, you start out with nothing, and you work hard, and you end up with homes and boats and children. That's the American dream, and I guess that we lived it. But it was a time when you could work hard and get ahead. I don't think the world is the same anymore. But you don't need houses and boats, or even children, to be happy. If you have your health and each other, life can be wonderful. Ours was. And I believe that even if we had not had the opportunities we had, we would have found a way to be content.

I decided early on that if I was going to support Harry, that meant I shouldn't say no to him. He was a soft-spoken guy, and he didn't ask for a lot. When Harry articulated something that he wanted or needed, I took

CHAPTER 3 :: YOU ARE WHAT YOU DO

it as an order! Not in a subservient way, but lovingly. Let's just say that his desires had a way of landing at the very top of the "to-do" tree.

He loved the ocean, so as soon as we could afford it, he asked for and got his boat. What was I supposed to do—lie on the ground and kick my feet over it? It made him happy, so it made me happy, too. And conversely, Harry was very lenient with me. He never thought I was out of line. Yes, I can be stubborn, and I can get angry and flare pretty brightly for a little while, but as far as my guy was concerned, whatever Barbara wanted, Barbara got. So I liked that—why should I not like that?

Until you've lived with another person, confident that he is going to support you before you even bring up your latest crazy scheme, you haven't lived.

Harry believed he could succeed, in part because I never doubted him. When he worked for himself, he never left the house without a big hug and a kiss and me telling him how wonderful he was. (When we worked together, that mushy stuff was just a part of our daily routine.)

When partners love each other, it makes life much easier. We didn't have big worries; we just had challenges that we faced together, and when success came to us, what was mine was his.

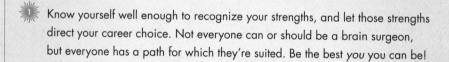

CUTIE'S COUNSEL

1 Know yourself well enough to recognize your strengths, and let those strengths direct your career choice. Not everyone can or should be a brain surgeon, but everyone has a path for which they're suited. Be the best *you* you can be!

2 Both people in a marriage need to feel free to pursue their passions, secure in the knowledge that their partners, even if they don't share the passions, will be supportive. Don't feel like you have to enjoy doing everything together or your life will become all compromise.

3 When you know your sweetheart has your back, you can reach for the stars and never stumble. Support the people you love, and watch them shine.

MAKING MONEY

Money makes the world go around, or so the song goes. Well, in my world, money is nice to have—but nicer still when you are in control of the money and not the other way around.

Money is an important commodity. You need it to pay your rent. It is a very important thing, but it is not *the most* important thing. Don't give money more power than it deserves.

I think that every couple argues about finances. After your children, it is the most controversial topic in any household. Unless both of you are Rockefellers, and maybe even if you are, money is more than just cents, green paper, and bank statements. It is emotional stuff, and it pushes everybody's buttons differently. You cannot run a house or a business without money, and you won't be able to do either happily unless you find a way to talk about what money means to you as an individual and how you are going to adapt so you can approach money as a member of a family and change your attitudes accordingly.

Money is like waves on a beach. If all is going well, the first wave will reach high enough to cover your basic expenses. You can afford a roof over your head, good food to eat, clean clothes to wear, gas and electricity, enough to cover your transportation to and from work—the minimum necessary so that you are not worrying every minute.

The next wave is for comfort. It reaches high enough that you can sock something away for a rainy day, invest in the children's college fund and for your retirement, treat your sweetheart to a new watch or yourself to a beautiful coat (I recommend a classic cut, in cashmere), take a trip, go out for a special dinner, donate to your favorite charity—all those extras that feel so good when you do them.

You'll notice that I don't tell you to save before you splurge. Money is for enjoying, when you can afford it, and I think a relaxed and pampered person is in a better position to get on with his or her life than one who is a workaholic with no room for play.

And even when you are able to splurge, never buy something expensive on a whim, unless you're in an auction house and the bidding is furious. Go away for a little while and think about it—there really is nothing so delightful as thinking about a wonderful item you wish to make your own. Do some research to ensure you are getting a good deal and that it is not a piece of junk. Weigh your options, and use your brains. That's what they're there for.

But let's get back to the beach. Now, as long as your wave is reaching high up onto the beach, you go right ahead and splurge or save (or both). But when the tide is still low, or God forbid, when it is very low, you have to conserve what you've got and make sure your budget is sensible and your expenses are contained. You don't shop for luxuries when the gas bill is late. It sounds so simple, but if you're at money's emotional mercy, you may not be able to see it or to control your spending. And if you're not dealing with money in a rational, healthy manner, I promise you, if it is not already affecting your marriage, it soon will.

If you are spending more than you are bringing in, that's a behavioral issue, and it needs to be addressed. It will not go away on its own. And nobody else is going to pay your bills. So grow up and become good with money. It is not a mystery. Anybody can do it.

If spending money you cannot afford gives you an emotional high, that's okay. Recognize it, and find an alternative high. Simply understanding what you're doing—and why—is going to make it easier to get back in control, and for me, being in control of my spending has always felt better than the momentary thrill of living outside my means.

Try daydreaming. It can be very satisfying, and it is the most inexpensive luxury I know.

Some people think they can use their money to buy love. Love is one thing that is not for sale. Don't be so foolish as to think that these two powerful commodities can ever be exchanged. The only people who try to buy or sell love are those who lack the ability to build love naturally. It doesn't matter how many lollipops I give you; you will never like me more because of them.

And the things that make me happiest—the feeling of the sunshine on my face, the sound of children laughing, the colors of the flowers, the smell of the sea—these things cost nothing. You can be happy just being alive and never have to put your hand into your pocket. It's all about your perspective.

Personally, I like working. It was always interesting, heading out into the world with my best face on and providing a public service. Every job I ever had was one that put me eye to eye with people who needed my help. I was never very concerned with how much I was paid for my time, although this was something that was always on Harry's mind. We are different people, and our approach to work and making money was different.

In today's world, unlike when I was young, it's not just the man who is working outside of the home and bringing back a paycheck. But although a husband and a wife might both go to work, it's very rare that they are equally compensated. For a long time, women have been paid less than men for doing the same work, and it has been harder for women to advance in business. That sort of situation creates stress and resentment for everybody— except maybe the boss who is getting a good deal by hiring women.

But it may be that in your family, the wife is paid more than the husband, which creates its own kind of stress and resentment. Or perhaps during the course of several decades, one of you will make more money and then the other will make more money. Every family is different, and there are no certainties except that work and money are a big source of stress for almost everybody.

But rather than getting annoyed because one person in the couple is well paid for every hour he or she clocks, and the other is only getting a fraction, remember that you are a team. The more successful half of the couple is acting on behalf of both of you, and all the money that comes into the house represents the household's income. If a man can make a lot of money, let him—or a woman, too! If you can make more money working together, that's best of all.

Even if you don't have a family business, when members of a family are earning a paycheck, that *is* the family business. That means that what one of you brings in belongs to both of you, to the family. In our house, Harry never said, "This is mine." He only said, "This is ours," and I did the same. He may have brought in more money than I did at various times, but that did not give him the right to be my boss at home. We would not have gotten along as well as we did if we let money take too big a role in our daily lives. What's important is that you respect and love one another and not let resentment over differences that you cannot control poison your affection.

We have always known people with money. If they were also smart, if they were kind, that's why we respected them. Money itself does not impress me. It's what you do to get your money and what you do once you've got it that are more interesting. I would be happy to sit down with you and hear all about these subjects, but if you want to talk about the size of your bank account, excuse me, I have a prior obligation.

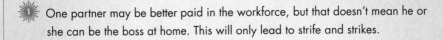

CUTIE'S COUNSEL

1. One partner may be better paid in the workforce, but that doesn't mean he or she can be the boss at home. This will only lead to strife and strikes.

2. If you can't cover the basics, forget about luxuries. Such treats should only be enjoyed when you're on an even financial keel, at which point, go a little nuts.

3. Love is love, money is money, and never shall they be exchanged. Don't even think about it. If you find that you do, take a break from romance until you break this dangerous habit.

SURVIVING FAT TIMES

When you are struggling and unhappy, it's easy to tell yourself, "Once these problems get resolved, I'm going to feel so much better," and to believe it.

Funny thing about bad feelings, though—they can be tricky and sneak up on you in ways you'd never expect. One of those tricks is how you can have the world on a string, all your ducks quacking happily in a row, and yet that sense of dissatisfaction is still right there beside you.

Just because your ship comes in, that does not mean that anyone will come down from heaven and swish all your problems away with a golden broom. Things have to come along gradually, and success brings as many challenges as failure does.

I think it's human nature to have episodes of unhappiness, and these don't necessarily have much to do with the reality of your day-to-day life. But if everything's objectively going great, it can be quite disorienting to realize that you've got the blues, and like a bad bruise, if you're not careful, those blues can turn purple on their way to turning black.

The answer to dealing with feelings of dissatisfaction isn't any different in good times than in bad: you just have to be honest with yourself, be willing to ask for help, and ensure that you don't lash out at the people closest to you.

There have been times when I've turned to my closest friends and vented like you wouldn't believe. There's no shame in expressing your frustration. All I wanted, and all I got, was a way to make me feel better and make my home a happier place to live in, and I think that I did okay.

Another danger when you're doing great is getting a swelled head. Good fortune is really only as good as how graciously you can accept it. So don't brag—especially not to anyone who isn't doing as well as you are. Don't start putting on the Ritz and squandering all that's come your way, because you might live to regret it. Don't dump your old friends, for good friends are awfully hard to find. Should you hit the jackpot, please stay levelheaded and be the person you have always been, just sleeping a little more soundly at night and being able to do a little more for the people you love, the charities you believe in, and, yes, for yourself as well.

And the most important thing about success is that it's not worth having if it means you must take something out of the other guy's pocket. Slow and steady, without infringing on other people, that's how we did it, and how you can do it, too. If the economy is bad, I promise you, it has been bad before, but it always does improve eventually. Don't try to fight the current of the economy. Read history and learn ways that other people have ridden out the bad times.

I think that if your ship comes in, it shouldn't alter the course you're already on. Money isn't so important that you ought to change everything about yourself just because you've got some. That would be like saying your old life wasn't any good, and I believe that you ought to have a life that you love, no matter how much you've got in the bank.

And while you're making sure you don't get spoiled, keep an eye on your sweetheart, too. He will help keep you in line, and you can do the same for him.

CHAPTER 3 :: YOU ARE WHAT YOU DO

I remember when Harry made a great business deal and was crowing about it, which was not like him. It rubbed me the wrong way, and I wasn't sure why at first. He was justifiably proud of leasing a big storefront—much bigger than we really needed for our shoe store—and being approached by a bank that wanted to sublease a big section of it for much more than we owed the landlord each month. And even taking the bank's space into account, there was still room we could sublease to a second business. We were both happy to know we'd have more money coming in, and it was Harry's doing that we had this stroke of good fortune, but I just didn't like how smug he was about the whole thing. So I sat him down and reminded him of where we'd come from and what simple people we were. I said that it was very lucky the bank had come along, but that was its doing, not his. We could have just as easily been stuck with a too-big storefront and all the aggravation that goes with that.

I didn't mind if he felt good about himself, but I wanted him to stay the sweet, humble guy I married and to recognize that luck and God had just as much to do with it as anything he'd done.

Basically, I am telling you not to be a jerk. A jerk is the guy who nobody likes, especially not himself. If you keep your feet on the ground, you'll be pretty happy no matter what the contents of your wallet are, and that will make you richer than any old Rockefeller you can mention.

True happiness comes from within, and as corny as it sounds, you will never be more wealthy than when you can look at the life you are living and feel proud of yourself for being a good person, a good partner, a good parent, a good member of your community. Maybe I'm crazy, but I think that being corny is cool. Give it a try and you may just find that you feel the same.

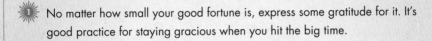

CUTIE'S COUNSEL

1. No matter how small your good fortune is, express some gratitude for it. It's good practice for staying gracious when you hit the big time.

2. There is no shame in feeling depressed, but if you try to hide negative feelings from yourself or those who love you, you're asking for trouble. Get some help if you are hurting.

3. Use your imagination to plan all the wonderful things you will do when you hit the big time. It's almost as much fun as actually doing them, and you'll have a blueprint to draw on if and when it happens.

HARDSHIPS AND CHALLENGES

STRESS POINTS

D o you want to hear something funny? Some people think, just because Harry and I were happily married for seventy-three years, that it was *easy* for us—as if we were magically suited to be contented together like a couple of cows in their pasture.

I am sorry to burst that bubble, but no, it wasn't easy.

As a matter of fact, there were even times when we thought about calling it quits. This was soon after we wed, before our children came along.

I was the firstborn and the big sister in my family, and I was used to calling the shots. Harry, who had grown up without a mother or much supervision at all, felt hemmed in by how domineering I could be—while at the same time recognizing that he longed for a caring person to hold his wilder impulses in check. Thinking back on that time, he said, "I needed somebody to hold me down on the straight path. If I didn't have Barbara to guide me through, I'd never have made it." Twenty-five when we married, he was still a bit girl crazy, and not used to anyone telling him what to do. But although he got sore and stormed off a few times, he always came back to me. At this early stage of our life together, he missed my companionship and our intense physical bond. Once he cooled down, he saw the merits of my opinions, and he dreaded the thought of losing everything we shared.

As for me, I didn't argue or chase after him when Harry pulled away, believing that if he really valued me and our partnership, he'd come back when he was ready. I give the same advice to women who e-mail me today wondering how to handle a husband in the grip of a midlife crisis or otherwise questioning his role: give him some room, and he'll either come back or you're lucky to be rid of him! There is no point in trying to keep alive a relationship in which both partners are not entirely committed to making a go of it. So if you have reason to doubt that your partner is committed, call his bluff and find out.

In our life together, I assure you that each of us had to overcome just about every little thing that can irritate, annoy, discourage, or dismay a partner—not to mention the really big problems that can break a marriage like a twig if you aren't very careful, very kind, and very quick to act when they appear.

We butted heads about sex, about keeping house, and about taking each other for granted. We disagreed about how to raise our children and how to spend our money. We quarreled about my family and about his, about where to go on vacation, and what to watch on TV. In this regard, we really were an average couple, but unlike some couples, we made a point of treating each one of these conflicts as an opportunity to negotiate and come to a peaceful place where we were both happy. We were always polite and respectful of the other person's point of view. Our perspectives might be different, but our goal was always the same: "Let's you and I figure out how to get through this problem together."

And just because we got through one of these stress points once, that didn't mean we could strike it off the list and gloat that at least we wouldn't have to go through that one again. Problems have a way of coming back to visit in new outfits, sometimes years after you've shown them the door.

Occasionally we would get through a very big issue so quickly and so smoothly that we almost couldn't believe it ourselves, only to have some trivial irritation work its way under both of our skins and just kind of *twist*. When that happened, we would get out the tweezers and operate. You can't let some dumb annoyance ruin the good feelings that every couple wishes to enjoy in their marriage.

Being married is a full-time, lifelong job—if you're serious about succeeding at it. You can't check out mentally and expect the carousel of romance to keep spinning and making beautiful music indefinitely.

I think the place where good marriages break down is when one or both parties begin to take the other person for granted. And yet it's understandable that this happens. Life is complicated and can be exhausting, so there is always a temptation when you get home to just tune out, because home is the one place where you *should* feel safe enough to let your guard down in this way.

But there's a difference between relaxing and disengaging, and while relaxing is a healthy way to recharge your psychic and spiritual batteries, disengaging is a drain on you and your relationships. Nothing is more important than that you recognize the difference and stay present for all the people that you love.

Yes, it's hard to be married. It's work to make your relationship succeed. I would not have wanted it to be any other way. Facing a challenge together and surmounting it feels good, and so does putting another candle on your anniversary cake and marveling at how much you and your sweetheart have been through as a team. Once we had been married for five years, we were looking forward to ten; and after twenty years, we felt that it would take a pretty big problem to even make a dent in the armor of our love for one another. Also, we would look around at our married or single friends, and much as we adored them, we would think, "Oh boy, I wouldn't want *their* problems—I think I'll stick with mine!"

The most important lesson that I can teach you from our happy marriage is that we did not rehash. If something was unpleasant, we got through it, handled the fallout, and did not bring it up again in happy times. So we both knew that once a problem was solved, that was it—we would not have to answer for it again, at least not in its current form. And knowing this, we could give all our attention to fixing the problems that came along, because once they were fixed, we could forget about them, which is a very wonderful feeling.

Conflict is a normal part of life, and you don't need to be afraid of it. Two people will almost always disagree on something, and this does not mean you're not meant to be in love or that your relationship is doomed. As long as you both are determined to respect one another and work through your conflicts promptly and with a smile, you are doing great. The best marriages can weather big storms and come through the other side with damp hair but big smiles.

CUTIE'S COUNSEL

1. Never ambush your partner with an old grievance. Work your problems out when they're fresh, forgive, and then move on with your lives.

2. It's fine to disagree, so long as you're nice about it. Contrary to popular belief, agreeing on everything is not necessary for a happy marriage.

3. Don't sit on feelings of resentment. If you feel you're being taken for granted, say so. Most problems of this sort can be cured with a little sunlight and fresh air.

FIGHT FAIR

It happens to everyone who has ever been in a relationship, and for each of us, it comes as a shock: all of a sudden, the warm, fluffy, and lovey-dovey feelings that have kept you blissfully uninterested in seeing fault in your sweetheart go away, and in their place, you find that you're feeling annoyed, or even angry.

There is no point in pretending it's not going to happen to you: it is. Smarter that you prepare yourself before the first fight happens, and make the promise to each other that whatever clouds will darken your days, you're both going to fight fair.

Maybe you grew up in a home where disagreements were unpleasant. Perhaps one of your parents used the threat of a meltdown to make the other people in the home do what he or she wanted. Maybe your parents didn't know how to communicate when they were upset. Or possibly they both pretended things were fine when they weren't.

Well, your childhood is really very interesting, and if you think so, too, you might want to invest in some self-help books or a therapist. But as a grown-up who has decided to connect with another person and form a new family, your responsibility now is to develop a healthy, honest, and effective way of handling the stresses and conflicts that are a part of every relationship.

So what does it mean to fight fair? Well, for one thing, there are no strict rules for how to handle your disagreements. Every person is differ-ent, so every couple is different, too. You must learn to understand yourself and your behaviors when you're upset, and you also must become very sensitive to how the person you love reacts in times of strife.

In our home, we learned how to get along by making mistakes that hurt each other. Maybe we made a mistake once, but we were never afraid to say, "I am sorry," and to make a mental note not to make that mistake again.

Once, when we were newlyweds, Harry was annoyed about something, I do not even recall what, and I snapped at him: "If you don't like it here, why don't you just pack your things and go?" I don't know where I picked up a phrase like that, probably from a trashy book or a movie.

To my absolute shock, Harry *did* pack his things, and he left me. I didn't know it yet, but you do not say things like that to Harry! He was gone for several days, and to this day, I have no idea where he went. Normally, I might have asked his sister, Lillian, the friend who had introduced us, where to find Harry, but it just so happened I wasn't getting along very well with *her* either—which maybe tells you that I was not completely without fault in this incident.

So I did what any young wife would do in these circumstances: for the first few hours, I felt very good about having stood up for myself, and for the next few hours, I felt very sad that Harry was still not home. Then I began to worry that something terrible had happened to him. When I couldn't stand it any longer, I went home to my mother and my father, and I cried until my pillow felt like a sponge.

Meanwhile, Harry was off thinking very seriously about if he wanted to put up with me anymore. He did come back a few days later, having decided that I deserved another chance. And I learned my lesson: Harry was not to be threatened. He did not care for ultimatums, and I would have to learn not to say terrible things in anger, because as far as he was concerned, being angry did not excuse me from being responsible for what came out of my mouth.

Well, I was willing to learn, and willing to change, because I sincerely did want us to get along better. If I had insisted on shooting my mouth off and told Harry that this was just the way I behaved when I was angry and

CHAPTER 4 :: HARDSHIPS AND CHALLENGES

he was going to have to learn to live with it, I expect that I wouldn't be sitting here writing this advice book.

What I said was serious, and what Harry did was just as serious. He got his point across, and although it hurt, it was effective, too. We both got that particular way of fighting out of our systems, and because I didn't suggest that he pack his things and leave again, he never had the occasion to do so.

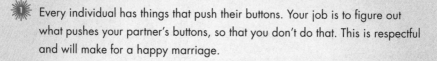

CUTIE'S COUNSEL

1. Every individual has things that push their buttons. Your job is to figure out what pushes your partner's buttons, so that you don't do that. This is respectful and will make for a happy marriage.

2. No matter how great the temptation, do not make big pronouncements when you're angry. Take a time-out, think, and cool off. Problems don't have to be solved in the moment, and very few are ever solved in anger.

3. Should your partner do something you find outrageous, it may be advisable to do something just as extreme—sometimes it's the only way you can get the message across about how upset your partner has made you.

WHEN PARENTS INTRUDE

When fate rolled the dice and cast Harry and I together, we caught a great many lucky breaks. One of the luckiest was that, unlike many young couples, we managed to begin our marriage in an atmosphere conspicuously lacking in family strife. Not every couple is so fortunate, but even if your extended family is difficult, there's no reason that you cannot find a way to coexist happily with them.

Harry did not have a large or close family. He had no mother. His father had died when he was in the service. His younger sister, Lillian, my friend who had introduced us, would soon marry and start her own family.

Actually, his older sister, Ruth, with whom he had lived when he came to California, didn't like me very much. I remember one unpleasant exchange when she chastised me for consulting my parents when we bought curtains. Apparently, she was the expert on curtain selection, which I did not know. Maybe if Ruth had stuck around, it would have meant more trouble in our family, or maybe we would have worked out our differences—I hope so. I never got the chance to find out, because she had a lung ailment and it killed her.

Then, back east, there were cousins, but out of sight, out of mind.

All this meant that Harry was starting our marriage with a clean slate. His sisters were happy to hear from him or see us once in a blue moon, but neither one had expectations of our new family playing a big part in their daily affairs.

Meanwhile, my family was a small one but very close and very kind. Our East Coast relations stayed where they were and didn't involve us in any drama. It was understood that on Sunday nights my mother would cook for everyone, that if we had troubles we would immediately seek their advice, that they were there if we needed a babysitter, and that the river of family love was strong and deep enough that Harry could jump right in and get as wet as anyone who happened to be a blood relation.

So in our home, there was never an argument over whose family would get to seat us at their Thanksgiving dinner, or which temple we would attend on the High Holidays, or, many years later, which deceased grandparent would be honored by naming a new member of the family after them.

My parents became Harry's new parents, by which I mean that they loved him like a son. I think that meant a great deal to Harry, because he had never experienced that kind of parental relationship. We all got along so well, and we spent a lot of time together. My mother and father lived into the 1970s, and until the day each of them died, Harry and I enjoyed a wonderful relationship with them, built on mutual respect, affection, and that indefinable thing that makes you feel at home with another person.

But this will not be a very helpful chapter if I spend it bragging to you about how lucky we were to have my delightful parents living just down the road, and no wicked stepmothers, or drunken uncles, or sets of baggage so heavy they almost snapped our backs. I've seen my share of families where the parent–child dynamic was not such a positive one, and I have some thoughts on what to do to make the best of the life God hands you.

Sometimes when my parents came to our house, they behaved as if it were their house—my mother in her ladylike way taking charge in my kitchen; my father giving orders, as was his habit. That's how it was in an Old World family, with the oldest male at the top of the totem pole. There was no question but that we would respect our elders, no matter what they said to us. They were entitled, through their greater age, to have opinions. So I was polite when my father was critical, and I was polite when Harry's sister was critical. Maybe later Harry and I would let off steam together, but in the moment there would be no tit for tat. We were all pretty happy playing the parts that we were given, because with a little bossiness came a lot of love.

There is a made-up Jewish phrase, "a real buttinski," and that's what my father was. Let me tell you, I never won a fight with my father. I don't think that anybody ever did. But, fortunately, Harry understood the situation from the start, and he didn't look for a battle. My father's behavior may have rankled, but not enough that Harry would make an issue and get between me and my parents.

The most important thing you must remember when you marry is that your husband or wife is now the most important person in the world—more important than your boss, the president, the pope, or your mama.

It doesn't matter what your respective family dynamics were up until the moment that the two of you exchanged vows, because as soon as you are married, the scales swing in a new direction. It can be hard for parents to understand this. It can be hard for *newlyweds* to understand this. But it's the most profound truth of any marriage, and as soon as you wrap your mind around this fact, you'll find it much easier to deal with any conflicts that arise.

In some families, two of the in-laws are easygoing, and the other set is demanding. There is a natural temptation to simply do what the demanding in-laws want, because that will keep them from squawking. This is a very bad idea. Why? Think about it. Yes, there will be less immediate conflict, but you and your spouse and eventually your children will end up spending a big chunk of your time as a family appeasing people who, if you had your druthers, you might not see very often. Meanwhile, the nicer in-laws, who don't raise a stink, miss out on the chance to spend time with you, and vice versa.

I don't believe in rewarding people for bad behavior. Individuals who bully do so because they usually get the results they are looking for. If you respond to their bullying with a gracious refusal and never sink to their level, in time they will learn not to waste their energy trying to intimidate you and will go off and pester easier targets.

There may be threats. There may be shouting. And if it's your parents doing the shouting, every part of you might want to give in, because you grew up getting your buttons pushed by these people. But if you can stand your ground—and use your new relationship with your spouse as the excuse for why things are now different—you will come out on top, eventually.

The only people who should have the final say in what is best for your family are the people who sleep in your bed at night.

However, some adults are really not ready to become independent of their parents. That is their own business, but it can become a problem if they try to have a mature relationship on the side. A Facebook friend wrote me for help because, after eight years, her "mama's boy" of a beau was still putting his mother ahead of their romance. I pointed out that although the mama might be irritating, my friend's real problem was with her boyfriend. I advised her to let him know that the situation was not acceptable because he was using his mother to prevent real intimacy from being established. At this stage, all she can do is put her foot down and see if any changes result. I am not a big fan of ultimatums, but sometimes they are the only way that a person can get the answer they need for their own peace of mind.

Another way that parents can be difficult is when they don't understand that their child has become an independent adult. I have known of mothers who still came over to redo their married son's laundry *after* his wife had already washed it, fathers who try to lay down the law on how their adult children spend their own money, and judgmental mothers-in-law who are outright rude to their daughters-in-law.

If one of these problems is yours, or if the parents in your life have come up with a completely new way of meddling, the answer is the same: all couples must learn to stand up for themselves, draw the line that they are comfortable with, and simply inform the parents, in a loving and empathetic manner, that this behavior is not acceptable.

If Mama comes in without knocking, change the locks. If Papa complains about the cost of your car, don't show him your bank statements.

Tell them how things are going to be different, and then *stick to your guns.* I promise you, even the most stubborn older person can learn new tricks. They have to, if they want to keep you in their lives, and, more important, if they want to have access to their grandchildren!

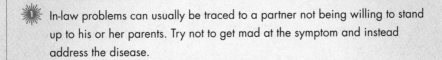

CUTIE'S COUNSEL

1. In-law problems can usually be traced to a partner not being willing to stand up to his or her parents. Try not to get mad at the symptom and instead address the disease.

2. A marriage reshuffles the family deck. Bride and groom are now Queen and King, and their respective parents are esteemed Jacks. King and Queen always win.

3. Should your families pressure your new family to do something you do not wish to do, tell them no, and stick to your guns. Learn to do this when you're young, and you'll save all concerned years of aggravation.

FROM LOVERS TO PARENTS

If you are planning to have children, mazel tov (that's Jewish for "hurray")! You are getting in on the most delightful business that two people can undertake together, one that will bring you such great satisfaction that you cannot even conceive of it until you experience it for yourself.

And you're also painting a big bull's-eye right in the heart of your relationship. Because when two people become parents, it is always a danger that the responsibility and the emotions and all that goes along with child rearing will swamp your love affair. If you're not careful, one morning you'll wake up to discover your kids are almost grown, and instead of a loving partner, you've got a coworker at a job that has nearly become obsolete. If that happens, it will be a huge and possibly futile effort to get your love affair back in order, even if both people wish it to be so.

But there are ways to keep the romantic spark alive through pregnancy and childbirth and up until your kids leave the nest. My advice is not so different from that I gave for dealing with a newlywed pair's parents. Your children are precious creatures and they will be the center of your lives together, *but they cannot always come first*. A family must have a hierarchy, and at the top of any family tree are the mother and the father. Their relationship is the reason that the family exists, and every member of the family must respect that relationship and recognize that it is a tender thing that must be protected, encouraged, and celebrated. I think that when a family is built around the idea of parents who adore each other, it teaches all members of the family how to show respect, how to value personal connections, and how to budget their time so that responsibilities get seen to and one's soul is also fed.

It's true that when your babies are small, there isn't much time left over for romantic gestures. But the wonderful thing about romance is that it is the quality, never the quantity, that matters. So when the baby is napping, throw a blanket on the living room floor, slice some peaches or plums or whatever you have in the house, pour a glass of something bubbly, and enjoy a mini picnic. If somebody is kind enough to offer to babysit, say thank you and make a date. Write love notes to each other and slip them in between the clean diapers. Be creative, and if you want your love to flourish, it certainly will do so.

As your children grow, do not pretend that you don't have a romantic relationship. Children learn from watching their parents, and parents are constantly shaping themselves through the way they behave around their children. Yes, you will be different at every major stage in your life: when you leave your parents' home, when you fall in love and marry, when you have children of your own, when your children move out. Your job is to be the best and most honest person you can be through all of these challenging changes. So what is the point of hiding the affection you feel for your spouse from the children? You must be comfortable in your home and able to be yourselves, tastefully expressing the love you feel.

In our family, it was me who was eager to have a baby. Harry would have been fine either way. But he wanted to give me the moon and the stars. Since I didn't want to own celestial bodies, he agreed to give me a little tiny person to play with instead. If I got pregnant, then he got pregnant. If I loved the baby, he loved the baby. So we loved the baby together and discovered what it meant to be responsible for a human life. Neither one of us had ever been responsible for even a pet before, and I would be lying if I didn't tell you it was scary, but also it was exciting. And the process of parenting—my caregiving at home, his hard work to ensure we three had all we needed—brought us closer. It was all we ever thought our lives together could be. It was not idyllic, but it was what we wanted.

I cannot explain why I wanted to be a mother. I just did. It seemed to me that I had spent my whole life growing, from a little child to a young woman. Being a mother was just continuing to grow. It felt natural and satisfying to me. As for Harry, even if parenting wasn't such a draw for him, once we had our children, he grew into the role of a father and was very comfortable there. We liked having children around. They were funny and sweet, and they needed us. They loved us, and we loved them. It was exciting watching them grow up, learn to do silly little things, start to express their personalities and ideas.

As our kids grew, it got harder to do things our way. Children have a funny habit of turning into people, and if they're your children, you'll find that they have a lot of your qualities, both good and bad ones. So perhaps it is simply a reflection of what Harry and I were individually that we raised a pair of stubborn, imaginative children who were pretty certain from an early age that they knew what they were doing.

It was not easy. I hate to feel tired and worried, and as a mother I often felt more tired and more worried than I had ever felt before. It was hard to keep an even disposition. You are kind of stuck with your own disposition, but you can also make the best of it. Learn to pace your activities, take deep breaths, and find a little space for yourself through the day so you aren't completely used up before dinnertime. Don't let anyone tell you that it's not hard work to be a parent.

But at the end of the day, when they were washed and smelling sweet, smiling at me from their pillows, I knew that there was nothing I loved more than being a mother.

I am sure that we spoiled our kids. (And if you asked Harry, he would tell you that he also spoiled me!) The war ended, and it was fun to be permissive, to buy them luxuries, and to send them out to enjoy life without having to worry about recycling every little thing as we had done during

FALL IN LOVE FOR LIFE

the years of deprivation. There were bicycles and sports cars and movie cameras, and plenty of soda pop in the fridge should they want to bring their whole class home for a pool party. There was money for college, and both our kids got good educations. We loved them very much and wanted them to be happy. Even when they were very bad, writing on the walls or tearing up their clothing, it was hard to say, "Don't do it!" They didn't like to be told no, and I didn't like to tell them no. If I could do it again, maybe I would be more restrictive—but if I had been more restrictive, I wouldn't have been me. Like Popeye says, "I yam what I yam." And I know that Harry and I did the best we could, making it all up as we went along.

By the time they were taller than us, we recognized that we didn't have much control over our children. We simply hoped that we had taught them well enough how to respect themselves and other people. Then almost before we knew it, they were out on their own. And all of a sudden, Harry and I were on *our* own, like we'd been in the first years of our marriage. Well, not exactly. Instead of a little flat and a handful of friends and no real clue of what we were doing, we had a home and a business and all kinds of habits, and a network of families who were part of our lives. Some of our friends had younger kids who thought of us as surrogate parents, and I know that our children felt similar bonds with some of our good friends.

I recommend that any young family try to build these kinds of relationships, which are very powerful and satisfying. You don't want to get so wrapped up in being parents that you forget to maintain grown-up friendships, because forming real friendships, like learning languages, is just easier when you're young.

Once a woman gets pregnant, she'll start running into ladies who are in the same position. Some of them will be nice, some of the nice ones will be interesting, and some of the nice and interesting ones will live in your neighborhood. You can make friends at the doctor's office, at the playground, at a Little League game, at ballet class, in the supermarket, at the library. Be friendly and interested in other people, and you are sure to find some that you enjoy very much.

If you can vacation with another family or several families, do so. It is more economical, and the parents can take turns watching each other's children. And as the years go by, the strength of such a support network is priceless. Our friends were there for us in hard times and in sweet ones, and they would always put us right if we had a bad idea. As our kids grew and made us worry, it was wonderful to have friends who understood what we were going through, who would listen to our troubles and support our decisions.

Being parents together is an incredible experience for any couple, but if you live a long, long life, like I have, those years of raising children will only represent a fraction of your experience, about the same amount of time you spent in school. You cannot be a schoolchild forever, nor can you be a hands-on mother or father forever. You must be a well-rounded person and continue to grow as an individual even as you are helping your children become independent.

My advice to young parents is to simply live your days one at a time, doing the best that you can. Listen to your heart, and to your partner's heart. If you make a mistake one day, don't panic; just don't make that mistake tomorrow. If you love your family, you want what's best for them, and that is precisely what you will get.

CUTIE'S COUNSEL

If you've got five minutes, that's time enough for a micro date with your sweetheart. Moments of romance will keep your love alive, so don't ever say you're too busy to drop everything and focus all your attention on the person you adore.

You will probably spoil your children, so don't deny that it is happening. If you recognize that you are spoiling your kids, also teach them good values along the way.

A family with kids should seek out other families in the same boat. These friendships can last for generations and mean a great deal to everyone involved.

THE NAG AND THE BRUTE

Men and women are different. Not better or worse—just different. Our brains are not wired the same, our moods don't affect us identically, and the hormones that flow through our bodies result in behaviors and feelings that distinguish the boys from the girls.

I enjoy being a woman, and I loved sharing my life with a man. It was exciting not to be on the same wavelength all the time and to bend a little so he could indulge in his masculinity, just as he would bend a bit so I could be more feminine. Couples who think they should only participate in activities that they both enjoy equally are really missing the point. As they say in my beloved Paris, *"Vive la différence!"*

Recently, a Facebook friend asked for my definition of a lady, and I defined a lady as someone who considers other people's feelings above her own and who is kind to her neighbors and to anyone she bumps into. I hope that I would have described a lady this way when I was thirty, but you learn these values as you get older. Maybe then I thought that being a lady had a little to do with kindness and a dash of fashion sense. I like the word *lady*. I know in modern times, people are concerned with misogyny and that all sorts of weak concepts are associated with all things feminine, but there is nothing better than a strong woman—and a strong lady is the best kind of strong woman. She respects herself and everyone around her, and she won't let anyone push her around.

Although every person is unique, certain qualities are typically thought of as characteristic of one sex or the other. Not all of these qualities are positive ones. I think it's important to be yourself, but at the same time, there is a risk in being *too much* yourself, to the point that you become obnoxious. And if a woman overindulges in the negative qualities generally characterized about her sex, her male partner may reciprocate by behaving unpleasantly masculine. My advice to you is to recognize these negative qualities, and your own tendency to act on them, so that you can better understand and control the impact that your actions have on the people who love you.

These gender stereotypes may exist in your relationship. I call them the Nag and the Brute. Many women have some Nag in them, and many men have a bit of Brute. The sooner you admit it, the sooner you'll be able to get a bit between your own Nag's or Brute's teeth and steer this person, and you, away from possible relationship disaster.

A Nag is a pest who judges other people and makes demands on their time. She has a special talent for grabbing onto an annoying subject at the worst possible moment and not letting go. A Nag won't take no for an answer, and she's never satisfied. Maybe she has a point, but she's so obnoxious that nobody can see it. A Nag wants to make other people feel as irritated as she does, and she usually succeeds.

A Brute is a big lug who expresses his power by refusing to interact or by yelling so loudly he scares the birds from the trees. He holds onto his resentments until small ones grow large, and by the time they do come out, it can be difficult for anyone to understand what he's so angry about. A Brute can be violent or simply intimidating. A Brute is stronger than those around him, but he might feel powerless. You can't reason with a Brute, and often it's easiest to just give in and hope he calms down.

Do you recognize either of these broadly painted characters in the mirror? If so, don't despair. It's possible to get a handle on your own nagging or brutish behavior and to improve your relationships with the Nags and Brutes who are close to you.

The first, and most important, step is simply to learn how to get outside the moment of any emotional upheaval that you're feeling and recognize what's happening. This is the case whether it's you that's acting out or whether you are on the receiving end. Nags and Brutes are people, too, and they're usually hurting. By responding with compassion, and breaking the rhythms of whatever dysfunctional tennis game you've both become used to playing, it's possible to stop this damaging behavior in its tracks.

If somebody is nagging you, listen to *what* she is saying—not how she is saying it and how annoyed you would normally be feeling. Then repeat it back, as a question, so she knows you're listening. "It sounds like you think I need to mow the lawn more often than I've been doing, and you feel embarrassed that the neighbors might be mad at us—is that right?" The Nag will probably be so shocked that you're paying attention that she will stop nagging. At this point, you can have a conversation about feelings and practical things that you both can do to resolve the problem.

If a Brute is upset and doesn't want to talk about it, respect that. Tell your Brute that you're so sorry he is upset, you hope he will feel better, and that you'll be there should he wish to talk later. If your Brute wants to go off and do his own thing for a while, don't fight it. I can't tell you how many times Harry disappeared into his garage workshop when he was in a mood and came back an hour or two later as his lighthearted self. Not that I was much of a Nag, but whenever two people live together, they are going to step on each other's tails.

In our home, we had what we called our honey-do list—"Honey, do this; Honey, do that." If there was something I thought needed doing, I'd add it to the list, and when Harry had some time, he'd go off and take care of it. Let me tell you, it's hard to get irritated at a man who is constantly showing up in your kitchen with a marker pen, striking one chore or another off your honey-do list! Sometimes Harry was so efficient that I had to struggle to think of new chores to add to the list. I only hope you will have such problems in your own marriage.

As for brutishness, I soon figured out how not to push my husband's buttons. He was an easygoing guy, but he didn't appreciate it if you leaned on him. When he stated his opinion about something important, that was his opinion, not a topic for negotiation.

I accepted Harry as he was, and he appreciated that. Other women he had dated previously had nagged, and when he told me he didn't like that sort of thing, I listened! And really, I didn't complain much, because basically I was satisfied. Some people are never happy with what they have, but I was not looking for much more than we had. I was delighted to be living with the man I loved, to be raising our children together, to see my parents regularly, to have enough food to eat, and cute clothes to wear. If there was something in particular that I wanted, instead of nagging Harry, I'd just talk to him. Funny thing, instead of getting mad and feeling pressured, he'd become the biggest advocate for whatever I was longing for, so long as it was reasonable. I guess we just worked well together.

Harry always said, "There are people and people and people." It's a funny thing to say, but you have to understand the context. If we had a customer in the shoe store who was a big complainer and who we realized could not be satisfied, "people and people and people" just meant not to forget that some folks are born with a storm cloud over their heads and the best you can hope for is not to get stuck in their mud puddle. We'd just smile and do the most for them that we could, within reason, and send them on their way as soon as we possibly could.

There are all kinds of folks in the world, and probably there is a partner out there for every one of them. If you're a big complainer, maybe you'll be happy with someone who also complains and who doesn't take all your bellyaching to heart. If you are a milquetoast, pick another just like you. For us, we wanted a calm and pleasant life. I didn't want him to be grumbling all the time, and he didn't want me to be picking at him, and it worked for us.

I think we got into some very good habits from the start, and I recommend that anyone thinking about getting serious about another person pick up such habits. It is easier to develop good habits than to break bad ones, and it is much easier to be happy when you lead with your head and your heart while watching your mouth.

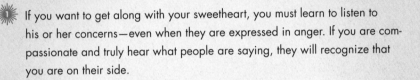

CUTIE'S COUNSEL

1. If you want to get along with your sweetheart, you must learn to listen to his or her concerns—even when they are expressed in anger. If you are compassionate and truly hear what people are saying, they will recognize that you are on their side.

2. Never demand an immediate resolution in a moment of upset. Be willing to wait until tempers simmer down to make peace, and you'll make much more of it.

3. Men and women, though very different, can be compatible. Don't beat yourself up for feeling a certain way, but do learn how to communicate. Compatibility is seldom naturally occurring, but it can be learned.

CHAPTER 4 :: HARDSHIPS AND CHALLENGES

SURVIVING AN INTERLOPER

One of the biggest threats to a happy marriage is infidelity. I know that this is so because many of the people who contact me seeking relationship advice are struggling with the aftermath of an affair—their own or their partner's. The pain and doubt resulting from affairs are terribly damaging, and many marriages do not survive them.

I think that very few married people set out to be unfaithful to their partners. But when a couple is having trouble—not communicating well or just not spending enough quality time together—an interloper can wiggle his or her way into one party's heart and make quite a big mess.

Once an affair has begun, there are many ways it can go, but every one of them is bound to hurt those involved. Better to work on the symptoms that cause affairs rather than trying to cure the disease after it has spread.

Some people get very upset if their partner flirts with other people, but I don't think flirting in itself is so terrible. What is flirting but connecting on a friendly level with another human being? As long as nobody takes it any further, a little flirtation is no big thing.

Sometimes if we were out shopping and I had been talking with a salesman, my friend would tell me that he had been flirting with me. Honestly, I didn't notice. Because I was not in the market for another man, all I saw in his conversation was friendliness and professional courtesy, both of which I enjoyed. If Harry had been there, maybe I would not have been quite as friendly. But any red-blooded woman feels pleasure when having a conversation with an attentive fellow. Flirting is harmless unless there is already a crack in your love affair. If there is such a crack, casual flirtations can quickly widen it, and before you know it, people are renting hotel rooms and sneaking around to use the phone.

The greatest enemy of affairs is honesty: honesty with your partner and honesty with yourself. Long before you are feeling lonely enough to enter into a physical or an emotional affair with someone else, you should be making a concerted effort to reconnect with your sweetheart.

If one of you has a job that keeps you apart for long hours, use your downtime to connect via e-mail or videoconferencing. Or be old-fashioned and write a love letter—it will be a wonderful surprise and something your beloved will treasure forever.

If you are not getting the intimacy that you want from your partner, you're going to have to talk about this, even if it's awkward or uncomfortable. Lack of intimacy is an issue that may be best solved with the help of a professional, since sexuality is such a charged topic, but don't despair—it can be solved, as long as both parties want to fix their problems.

Most couples who are having major problems end up in couples counseling, but therapy isn't just for people who are trying not to split up. Many faiths recommend or even require couples to take part in some premarital counseling as a prerequisite for getting married, and I think that an occasional visit to a sympathetic professional can help even the happiest of couples to stay that way.

After Harry and I had been married for forty years, we went away for a "Marriage Encounter" weekend after hearing friends rave about their experiences. This was a group activity meant to enhance our relationship and deepen our connection, and I think we both got a lot out of it. We participated in guided discussions with other couples, learned some new coping mechanisms, and worked separately on a love journal in which we confessed the things we most loved about our partner, the things that we found challenging in our marriage, and how we intended to improve them.

CHAPTER 4 :: HARDSHIPS AND CHALLENGES

When we got home, we told everyone how interesting it had been, and we wondered why we hadn't done something like this before. I think even for a couple that doesn't have a lot of problems, just spending two whole days focusing 100 percent on one another and the relationship is a wonderful vacation. Making time to enjoy each other without distractions is a great way to strengthen your bond.

It is interesting for me to look back at the journal I kept at that "Marriage Encounter" retreat. Most of it was a long letter to Harry in which I opened my heart. These are the things that a happy wife thinks about but does not always tell her husband. I am glad that we were encouraged to express our true feelings. Let me share a few of the less private things that I shared with Harry, to give you a sense of the emotions that were stirred through these exercises.

As for you and me, we've really got it made. You married the girl you want, and I married the boy I want. You were never envious and we never set our sights too high, so we were always delighted with whatever good fortune came our way.

There is nothing I want that is not what I want for us both.

You've built up my ego and have made me feel bright, beautiful, wanted, and endearing. That is a great gift. The best, really, for how could I have managed without it?

When I seek to hold your hand is the time when I'm afraid, bewildered, or have reached the end of my endurance. And then I need to hold your hand to feel that I'm not alone and that hopefully you can share my problem and help me know that you're there and understand my needs. Very often at night before going to sleep, I hold your hand, and I feel like saying, "It's been a long road and we've made it. Some of it has been rough, but then some of it has been great." Love, Barbara.

So that is what "Marriage Encounter" helped me to express—the loving and appreciative feelings that I was holding inside but should have been sharing with Harry all along. He was grateful to learn of them, as I was to hear him articulate how much he loved me. Our relationship was different, better, after this weekend away.

Some people have affairs because they want to end their relationship but lack the courage to tell their partner. So they simply go out and start a serious new relationship and are careless enough that it doesn't stay a secret. When their partner finds out and blows a gasket, the cheating spouse slinks off to his or her new sweetheart's arms, having gotten what he or she wanted all along. Of course, one cannot trust a person who has begun a relationship prior to ending his or her last one not to do the same thing all over again. "Buyer beware," in love and in retail.

Some people have affairs because they tell themselves that they deserve more attention than they get at home. Or maybe they are annoyed because they do not feel all of their needs are being met by their partner. Well, whoever told them that one person could meet their every need? You can actually live quite comfortably without having all your needs met—try thinking about it that way; you might be surprised at how liberating it is. You are not perfect, and neither is your partner, but you can make a very pleasant life together if you are both serious about providing the love and support that go along with a marriage.

Sometimes an affair will come out into the open, and the cheating partner will beg for forgiveness. It is up to each person to determine if he or she is willing to forgive and forget, and it is up to each cheater to determine if he or she can control his or her behavior. Thank God, I did not ever have to make the decision, because I don't know if I would have been able to forgive. I loved Harry, but I also loved the idea of him as my true, faithful love. Although I am open-minded about how other people live, personally, I am a very square lady. If it had become obvious that he was not what I thought he was, how can I say how I would react?

My opinion is that if Harry had cheated and I had caught him at it, he would have cooked his own goose. I might have forgiven him one time, but I am pretty sure I would not have forgiven him the second time. And most cheating husbands are repeat offenders.

I am not naive. I know what men are like and that they are not all true blue. But I honestly believe that Harry was not a chaser. I spent a great deal of time with him, at work all day and then home in the evenings, and I never saw signs that he had a secret life or that there were things he needed but was not getting from me. If he thought about other people, he did not advertise it. If he acted on such thoughts, it did not show.

Maybe you are married to a cheater, you know it, and you decide you do not mind. Some people are like that: they settle for what they settle for. Maybe you love your partner enough to let him or her run around, or maybe you *don't* love your partner all that much, so it doesn't matter what he or she does. If you find yourself with a repeat offender, you have big problems, and my sympathy. Although I believe in working hard to make a marriage work, sometimes a person just has to do what is best for him- or herself as an individual, which might mean walking away from someone you feel you can no longer trust.

But what if you are in a pretty good marriage that has been impacted by one partner's possible affair? If you are the innocent party who suspects infidelity, and you wish to keep your marriage together, all you can do is to go to your partner and say, "Honey, there are some things we've got to straighten up."

Then try to find out what has been happening. You will need to use all your wits and intuition as you judge your partner's response. Is your partner contrite and honest with you when confronted? Does he or she deny that anything is wrong, even though you know something is? Does he or she confess to some but not all of the behaviors? You cannot fix a broken marriage without shining a light on the break, so take a deep breath and reach for the light switch. It is scary, but I think when you are ready to really look at the situation, you will find that you are tougher than you realize.

Not long ago, a woman asked me for advice on how to rebuild the trust in her thirty-year marriage after she did something that her husband did not wish to forgive. I reminded her that it takes two people to make a relationship work, and if she had made a sincere effort to make things better, the ball was still in her husband's court. You cannot force someone to forgive you. If two people cannot solve their problems after such an effort, it might be time to close the book and start all over again. And although this relationship may end, that does not mean she has to give up on love. There are new relationships on the horizon in every life, and just because a marriage may be ending, that does not mean that there cannot be love or happiness in the future, as long as you look after yourself and don't make the same mistakes next time.

A strong relationship can survive an affair, but the strongest relationships never have to weather that storm. Stay in touch with yourself and your partner, and don't be complacent about what you have together, and you will have a good chance of avoiding this threat to your happiness. In the meantime, flirt a little, love a lot, and be good. In my experience, being good is much more fun than being bad.

CUTIE'S COUNSEL

✳ Make time in your busy life for romantic getaways during which you focus on the relationship and each other. Turn off the cell phones and leave the computer at home. You'd be amazed what just a night or two away from it all can do for your love life.

✳ Courting lovers send written messages, but settled couples seldom do. Make a point to write letters sharing your true feelings throughout the relationship. Your partner will cherish them forever, and if they're not *too* spicy, so will your children and grandchildren.

✳ If you have wronged your partner, get used to the fact that he or she will be very upset, and you cannot control someone else's feelings. You will have to accept complaints, and you have no right to object. If you don't like it, behave better in the future.

✳ A floundering relationship cannot be saved unless both parties are sincerely committed to its rescue—and even then, it is not a sure thing. Be certain that both you and your partner are on the same page before investing too much time in a damaged relationship.

LIVE, LOVE, AND ALWAYS LAUGH

You might as well admit it: there is a long list of challenges that can try the patience of any couple, and the odds are that if your relationship lasts longer than a couple of seasons, you'll have a chance to experience a great many of them. That can sound overwhelming, but you should not be discouraged.

The nice thing about challenges is that they don't usually hit all at once—although sometimes it might feel that way. But I have found that the universe doesn't give you much more than you can handle. As a problem appears, if you are reasonably prompt in dealing with it, you'll be in good shape before the next bit of trouble rolls along. And as you work through problems with a partner, the two of you become closer and more in tune with each other. Your past troubles give you something to talk about and a sense of accomplishment that is hard to beat.

If you think of your life as just a series of problems to be solved, you're going to be pretty anxious. I prefer to look at problems as speed bumps on an otherwise smooth and open highway—and as long as this is my metaphor, I might as well imagine that I'm driving in a little red convertible with my driving gloves and sunglasses on. Pretty cute, aren't I?

So once in a while you hit a speed bump, but as long as you don't drive recklessly through life with bare tires and loose bumpers, no little old speed bump is going to run you off the road. See it, recognize it for what it is, deal with it, and move on. That is my advice for anyone facing a problem.

Troubles come when you don't follow these simple directions. Ignoring a problem, pretending it is something else, refusing to do anything about it, wallowing in your pain—these are all recipes for allowing a relatively minor issue to blow up and take over your life. Don't let problems rule you; take control of them instead.

But some problems aren't speed bumps; they're huge, gaping holes waiting to swallow you up. I'm thinking about one of the worst things that ever happened to Harry and me, the death of our first son, Jerry.

He was just a baby, and he had some breathing problems, and at the time, there was really nothing the doctors could do. They just sent him home with us, and we hoped for the best. He was a good baby, and we loved him a lot. And then he died.

My God, you cannot imagine. Or maybe you can, if it has happened to you. It's more common than you might realize until you experience it, and sympathetic people come up to share their stories of loss.

So there we were, still newlyweds, practically strangers, very much in love with one another and with our son, and all of a sudden there were just the two of us, and this huge, aching wound, and no instruction manual for what to do next. I felt like I was going to die, but I didn't die. I asked God why, but he did not answer. So I did the only thing I could do: I went on.

Everybody grieves in his or her own way. I know that some couples don't survive the loss of a child. Maybe they blame each other, or they find that they can't look at their partner anymore without seeing the absent child. If Harry had felt that way, it would have broken my heart, but I would have understood.

Thank God, he did not.

We didn't talk much about it, but we leaned on one another in a quiet way. We mutually understood that we were going to feel our pain but not define ourselves by it. I knew that Harry was hurting, and he knew I was, too. Simply by staying together, we supported each other through the worst of it.

In time we had a little daughter, and then a second son, and our lives were very full raising them, and then our grandchildren. We never forgot the child we had lost, but we didn't dwell on him. The pain would not have been any less if we had kept picking at the wound, and we never felt that by not talking about him we were in any way forgetting or denying how important he had been in our lives.

I guess we could have split up and forgotten we ever had a child, but I'm awfully glad we didn't. We stuck it out for about seventy more years, until our son, had he lived, would have been an old man.

And then I lost Harry, but the funny thing is that he's still here with me. I hear his voice and see his smile and feel his arms around me. After so many years, we are really the same person. We are not separated—it's not as if he was with somebody else, or that he wants to be elsewhere. He didn't have a choice. He isn't here physically, but for me, that doesn't matter. And again I thought when he died that I would die, but I didn't. If God is keeping us apart, okay; who can yell at God? Maybe as long as I'm alive, a big part of Harry is alive, too.

So there are speed bumps and there are tiger pits. Life isn't so easy, but I think we can agree that the alternative is worse.

You've got to keep a sense of humor if you're going to survive in this life. We're all ridiculous. We get into silly fights with friends and relations and let them drag on long after we no longer feel angry. We forget to take care of important matters, and then we panic when we realize it's too late to do so. We break and lose things. We misjudge. We're human, and these are simply the human foibles that we have to accept in ourselves and in the people we love. If you expect perfection, you'd better fall in love with a computer, because people have flaws—or quirks, if you wish to be kinder in the words you choose.

So if you want to thrive through good times and bad, I suggest that you practice your belly laugh. Learn how to see the funny side in the darkest moments and to laugh at yourself most of all. Nothing is better at breaking the tension. It's like your body is a whip and it just got snapped.

And if you feel blue, don't wallow in it. Put on a Marx Brothers movie, or listen to a recording of your favorite comedian. Play with a puppy, if you've got one. Watch a Bugs Bunny cartoon, or Monty Python, or whatever brand of humor tickles your fancy. I find that even a few minutes of laugh therapy can completely reset my mood and give me a new perspective. If I don't have a movie or record or book or puppy close at hand, I just close my eyes and think about something amusing, or make a face in the mirror, and that does the trick. Laughter lightens the mood, and I think most of us could benefit from that once in a while.

In those moments when either Harry or I got all wrapped up in an excess of irritation, it was our habit to break the tension with some playful teasing. He always knew what to say, or the perfect silly face to make, and my big grumpy balloon would just go *pop!*

If you know another person very well, you know the shortcuts to connecting with him or her. When we were newlyweds, we didn't yet have this talent, but as our relationship grew and deepened, it became easy for us to recognize when our partner was having a hard time and to help each other in a way that was respectful but also lighthearted. And to be honest, I think we got a lot closer in the aftermath of our son's death. So that was a terrible thing, but it was also key to making our marriage as strong as it became.

If Harry was blue, he didn't want to feel that way, and I agreed with him. So if he wanted to feel better, and I wanted him to feel better, what would be the point of me getting mad at him just because he was feeling sad? If I wanted him to snap out of it and he refused, and I got mad and he got more stubborn, and I yelled at him and he stormed out of the house, neither one of us could be called the "winner" of that argument. It sounds ridiculous when you spell it out, but this is a vicious cycle that many couples perpetuate and one that ends up with two unhappy people rather than the one you started with, or the zero we liked to end with.

There are many things you can do to get yourself out of the dumps. Try a change of scenery. Engage in some lively physical activity. Play with your pets. Call a friend and listen to *her* problems for a change. Some people like to bang on a drum; others want to sit quietly in the sunshine. Find the thing that works for you, throw a little laughter into the mix, and I think you'll soon find you're feeling like a new person—or like the old one you were missing.

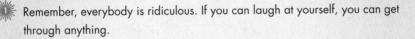

CUTIE'S COUNSEL

Remember, everybody is ridiculous. If you can laugh at yourself, you can get through anything.

Problems will not disintegrate if you ignore them; they will find others and build a nest in your life. Deal with your problems when they're fresh, or it will be much harder to eradicate them.

Not every issue requires conversation. Sometimes it's enough to just quietly be together and demonstrate your care for one another through body language.

When your own troubles are wearing you down, go find a friend and listen to *her* troubles for a change. You will both be the better for it.

Chapter 5:

GROWING OLD
TOGETHER . . .
AND GOING ON ALONE

WHEN CHILDREN BECOME ADULTS

It's a funny thing, being a parent. When you start, you don't have the first idea of what you're supposed to be doing, but you jump right in and you figure it out. Babies are pretty easy; teenagers not so much. But with love and patience, you raise your children the best you can, and much sooner than you expected, they are off on their own doing whatever they want, with no parental supervision except what they have internalized.

Well, there's no point in worrying, then. All you can do is keep loving them and hope you've done a good job teaching them to respect themselves and other people. They are going to live the lives they want to live, and from now on, you get to watch but not to steer.

As they got bigger, sometimes we worried that our kids would go off in a bad direction, and we wondered if it would mean we hadn't done a good-enough job. You would be amazed how much worrying parents can do at night if one or both of them should have a bout of insomnia. On such nights, I recommend warm milk and a book. A little worrying about your kids is normal, but eight hours of it can drive anyone around the bend.

I won't say that our children were perfect, but neither were we. We all had our ups and downs. Your children tend to be a lot like you, which means if you are stubborn, they can be more stubborn, and in exactly the same ways. But whatever we disagreed about, we always loved each other. And I always thought that my kids were smarter and more interesting than anyone else's kids, and I still do.

I think that if a mother is honest, she will admit that she liked her children better when they were small. I certainly did. They were young and innocent, and they still belonged to me. When they become adults, they have an outside interest—their own independence. It is a rare mother and child who do not struggle making this transition. Every parent should prepare themselves because it is going to happen to you, and when it does, it is going to be a challenge.

Independence doesn't mean that children are ready to live on their own. It happens much earlier than that, in stages. It begins when they start thinking for themselves instead of going along with what the family—by which I mean Mama or Papa—wants. And as a parent, you have mixed emotions, because you are proud to see your little one taking these important steps toward adulthood, but independent children can be incredibly trying. They demand to know why they must do the simplest things, or they sulk, or they slip off when you're looking for them and make everyone worried. They can be very rude and hurtful, or they can be so sensitive that the slightest remark sets them off into hysteria. If anyone ever tells you that raising children isn't the hardest work in the world, you have my permission to blow a juicy raspberry in their direction.

But eventually, God willing, every child is going to become an independent adult. That is why you bring them into the world, and it is not something you could or should fight against. As they grow up, all children get to figure out what really matters to them. They break away from some family patterns and traditions, but other ones they hold close and make part of their grown-up lives. If you can distance yourself from it enough to look objectively, it really is a fascinating process. And what you hope, what all parents hope, is that when they do find their own path, it will be one that is compatible with yours.

A Facebook friend wrote to me asking for advice on dealing with the terrible teens, which might be the most challenging time in a parent's life. I told her to remember that she is a human being, too. Teenagers have all kinds of feelings and are going to act out however they do. In the midst of that, a mother needs to keep perspective and enjoy her own life. Parents cannot live for their children. All children need to make their own mistakes, fall on their own fannies, and dust themselves off again. If you can make sure your children know they can count on you for the truth and your love, then they will be well on the way to finding their way in the world. It is a delicate balancing act, to be there for them without losing yourself—but it can be done.

And as your children grow up, they need you less, which means you have more to give to yourself, and your partner, and the other people you love. That is an important thing, since the transition you make away from being a caregiving parent will shape the person you are going to be for the rest of your life.

There is no magic bell that rings to tell you and your kids that they are now grown-ups. Some children are adults when they are twelve. Others never become adults. When they move away from home for the first time, that's a pretty significant moment. I recommend waking up to a house without children for the first time to all who want to make sure their tear ducts are in working order. But, thank God, our children never moved too far away. And they weaned us off of living with them by going away to college and coming home for the holidays.

Some parents and children never do quite cut the cord. The young people might never move away from home, or perhaps they do move out but remain tightly tethered to their parents in other ways. Our son Jan was the child who stayed closest to us, while our daughter, Carol, went off and did her own thing for much of her life. I was always proud that our children developed into thoughtful and curious adults who pursued their passions, yet I was troubled that, in our family, we all dealt with the fallout from sibling rivalries well into Jan's and Carol's middle age.

The best thing Jan ever did for me was to give me grandchildren. Eventually, I got to have seven of them—*seven!* I have a lot to say about being a grandmother, but for now, suffice it to say that I am a big fan of the institution.

My kids were independent thinkers, and they lived life their way. They came of age in the 1960s, which couldn't have been more different than the time when Harry and I were growing up. Where we had to worry about unemployment and the war, they worried about free love and weird drugs.

Of course, they had a war to worry about, too, and one day Jan decided he was going to protest it. He got arrested, and we were so worried about him that we decided to let him cool his heels for a little while before we bailed him out. He must not have enjoyed the experience, because although he didn't stop talking about his opposition to the Vietnam War, he didn't participate in any more sit-ins after that.

I think that parents experience something like growing pains when their children leave the nest. The protective attitude that it has been your duty to express becomes inappropriate, and if you don't want to make your children mad, you must stifle the urge to fret over them or to tell them what to do. All of a sudden, you must treat this formerly little person as an equal. Your children will teach you how important it is to change your behavior, because if you treat them like children, they will throw a childlike tantrum and storm out the door. And the worst part of it is . . . they're right!

So a good parent must agree to stop being such a mama or a papa all the time and to become something of a friend to her or his children. You have to respect their independence and hold your tongue, although when you see them about to make a big mistake, of course you will have something to say. You have to learn how to say you're sorry for overstepping your bounds, but you also have to be available whenever your grown-up child comes home with a boo-boo and wishes to be your little baby again. All in all, it might be more difficult letting your children go than it was to raise them in the first place.

A big challenge for me as a parent was watching our son's first marriage fall apart. He and his wife had two little girls, Kim and Spring, whom we adored. We understood that Jan and his wife had grown apart and that they would probably both be happier if they split up, but we worried a lot about how their separation would impact the children.

The notion of a couple being incompatible or having nothing in common was pretty alien to Harry and me. We didn't know whether we had things in common. We lived together, we ate together, we slept together, and we worried together. Presto—we were compatible. But such was not the case for our son and his wife. I think they just outgrew each other. They were very young when they married, and with time, they figured out that they didn't want the same things. Actually, my son was still trying to figure out what he wanted when he was sixty. Some people are like that, and it's a challenge to share that path.

All we had ever known personally was intact families, but divorce was becoming very common in the 1970s. We had friends whose children were in the same boat, so we commiserated. We did not question Jan or blame him or tell him they must stay together for the children's sake. There is no point in trying to tell your adult children how to live. If you have an opinion, and you are fortunate, maybe they will listen to you. But they are entitled to make their own decisions, including those we might think are poor ones. Of course, when we thought one of our kids was about to make a very bad decision, we would try to get our thoughts across, but ultimately, every person is responsible for his or her own life.

So when we saw that the divorce was inevitable, we just prayed that everything would work out, and we made ourselves available to the girls. As it turned out, they would spend much of their childhood years with Harry and me, which we all enjoyed. It isn't what anyone involved hoped for, but I think that our family made the best of it, and the result is that I have a very special bond with my granddaughters that I would not give up for anything.

You should not be a parent if you are not prepared to let your children go. Once they are in the world, they are going to find their own way. Sometimes it is very hard to watch them do things the way they choose to, but you must learn not to criticize and be accepting. You probably did things your parents weren't so pleased about, but if they were very good, you might not have ever known how much they worried about you.

All of my children are gone now. We lost Jerry when he was small, and then within six months of one another, in 2007, our daughter, Carol, died and then our son Jan.

Neither of these deaths was expected, and it was a terrible shock to the system. We certainly never planned to bury all of our children. I can ask God why this happened, but God never answers when you ask such questions. I simply try to be grateful for all the years and the memories that we had together and to keep in mind that God has a plan for all of us. Harry and I had already survived the death of our first son, so as heartbreaking as it was to lose our other children, we knew that we could live through the pain and that it would get better. We did live through the pain, and it has gotten better, but I miss my children. I hope that someday I will see them all again.

CUTIE'S COUNSEL

 Always remember that your children will be adults one day. Practice mutual respect from the start, and they may even grow up to be your friends.

 Trust that your kids are strong enough to make their own mistakes, to survive them, and to learn from them. A coddled child never spreads his own wings but waits for you to do the things all humans must do for themselves if they are going to grow and evolve.

 A well-raised child may brave rough seas, but like a well-crafted ship, they will right themselves in the end. Good parents know how to let their children discover for themselves that they have what it takes to make it in this world.

GRANDCHILDREN: THE REASON WE HAD CHILDREN

For nearly half my life, when somebody asked me to tell them about myself, one of the first phrases out of my mouth was "I am a grandma!" Some little girls dream of being mothers. I loved being a mother, but once I became a grandmother, I knew that I had found my calling. I recommend it to everyone.

You cannot be a grandparent unless you first have a child, and then it's up to your child if he or she is going to make you a grandparent or not. Since child-free lifestyles are quite popular today, it may behoove you to have several children in order to increase the chances that you will be a grandparent—though, of course, such a decision will have its own consequences.

But if God and your children do not give you grandchildren, don't despair. The world is full of wonderful young people who would like a grandparent in their lives, and you can build strong relationships with neighbors' kids, extended family, or through a volunteer program like Big Brothers or Big Sisters. I am a grandma, but I also have known some surrogate grandchildren who have greatly enriched my life.

Harry and I had two children who grew into adulthood, and only one of them had children of his own. We were blessed, but we would have accepted it if our children had not wanted to be parents. This is not something you can nag another person about—it is too private. Some people do not want the burden of the financial responsibility or to give so much of themselves. Some people do not meet the person who they can see having a child with at the right time. Some people want children but cannot conceive. We all have different needs and different lives. I think that it is important to respect each person and not try to make him or her fit inside a box.

But I am happy that my son chose to have children and to share them with me. There's just something special about connecting with a small person at the stage in your life when you are probably feeling very comfortable about who you are and where you're going. It is different from becoming a parent when you are a young person yourself. There isn't the same level of responsibility, and if you've already been through it, you are not so worried about accidentally breaking the child or doing something wrong. It's all the pleasures of parenting without the anxiety.

Most ladies would be frantic at the thought of turning fifty years old, but, lucky me, I was so excited about the impending birth of my first grandchild that I barely noticed that big birthday come and go. Her name was Kim, and she was a wonderful birthday present.

It was great to have a baby in the family again, but the real fun came as Kim started talking. She decided to share her dreams with me, and I was happy to hear them. I do not know why we bonded so strongly, but we did. I had the privilege of playing a big role in her life as she grew, and because I was there for important milestones like the first day of school and learning to swim, she came to see me as a sort of third parent.

Kim is a very sophisticated young lady. She is knowledgeable, and she is not a softy. She does not bend easily. I respect Kim's opinions. She is very, very straight. She had a million questions, and she thought I had all the answers. I have always done the best that I could to not disappoint her.

After Kim came her sister Spring, a beautiful and very loving child. She is a lot of fun and very charming. She can laugh at herself, which is a nice quality. She is not as serious as Kim, but I think she is equally smart. She lives in the moment, and I love her personality. She too connected strongly with me, and I have always thought of her as my own daughter and tried to give her the things that a mother should. Their parents did not have a solid marriage, so it was up to me and to Harry to fill in the gaps. That was not such a happy circumstance, but we were glad to step in, and we found it very rewarding to help our girls thrive.

Two decades later, to my surprise and delight, my son Jan remarried, and he and his second wife had five more children. So I got the pleasure of welcoming another granddaughter, Chinta Tina (named for my mother, Tina), into my life. She is another charming child. She has a quiet kindness in her. She doesn't really show her emotions, but you can depend on her for life. She does not judge. She will never tell you a lie, and she never exaggerates.

Next came my four handsome grandsons. The eldest boy, Morgan, is a very intelligent young man with a passion for the arts. He is the leader of his younger brothers and holds himself apart from the crowd. Robin is the oldest of the twins, a good listener with a fine sense of humor. His twin brother Dylan is more introspective and thoughtful. Harrison is the youngest, and he wants to be like his big brothers. He is affectionate, likes to try new things, and is in tune with his emotions.

If you meet them, I think you will like my grandchildren.

Grandchildren are great because they help you stay relevant. You can feel young, vicariously, through your connection with them and participate in very silly activities that you could not get away with as an adult without a child by your side. Smashing Silly Putty onto the Sunday comics? Playing a round of miniature golf? Placing marshmallows into the microwave to see what happens? Sign me up!

Children are naturally curious and energetic. They ask interesting questions and have infectious, if sometimes weird, enthusiasms. They are bouncy, smiley, and sweet, and they give great hugs and too-wet kisses. They are very accepting when you make a fuss over them, and my grandchildren grew up to be respectful, industrious, and all that you could want. Can you tell that I am a fan?

I know some people think that once they've raised their own children, they are no longer responsible for the little ones in their family, but I never felt it was an imposition. Your children are your children, grand or not. I don't know where it stops or ends. I felt drawn to be with them, and so I was. If I needed the energy, I found it somewhere—when I was in my fifties and then again when I was much older. I tried to be the best grandmother I could be, and as long as the children respected me like I respected them, I was happy to give of myself. I loved them and hoped to see all of them stand on their own two feet and head out into the world. That is the reward of the grandmother.

Sometimes people ask me my secrets for being a good grandma. Obviously, they have not yet had grandchildren of their own or they would know that there aren't any secrets, just a lot of common sense. Your job is very simple: to love them, to nurture them, to support them, and to enjoy them. You must simply accept their points of view, be patient and listen, and always be truthful. Children can smell a phony a mile away, so talking with a grandchild has a way of keeping you honest—with the child and with yourself. I happen to find this refreshing, but you might not agree. Children have a way of innocently blurting out things that embarrass the grown-ups within earshot, but I have always found this quite funny, even when the joke is on me. Little children don't yet have shame or self-consciousness. I think this is a joy to see.

Not all grandmothers are lucky enough to live in the same area code as their grandchildren. A Facebook friend wrote asking me for ideas on how to be a long-distance grandmother, which was something new for her. I suggested that she visit the post office. A letter from a grandmother is something special to look forward to, even more now that people are so comfortable with the idea of instant communication. By the same token, a weekly telephone call can be a special date that everyone anticipates. Hearing each other's voices is a powerful experience, and so is getting something physical in the mail. And during those calls, take time to really listen to your grandchildren and let them know how much they are loved,

173

and the miles between will simply melt away. I think that mere distance cannot break the bond between grandparents and their grandchildren. As long as you continue to make your family your priority, you will still be their grandma, today and forever.

I enjoyed all my grandchildren when they were small, but I didn't really think about how our relationships would evolve as we all got older. Even though I thought of all the girls as my daughters, I did not expect that they would think of me as a mother and as someone for whom they would make personal sacrifices when I needed help.

I also did not anticipate that all my children would die before me. But they did.

And so, to everybody's surprise, after her father died, there was a new oldest "child" in my family. This was Kim, who was then forty years old and newly married to her sweetheart, Richard. When we needed help getting our lives in order, it was Kim and Richard and Kim's littlest sister, Chinta, who took the lead to make that happen, and we let them know we were very grateful. This is how our family has changed, and all I can say is that we have been lucky. We did not spoil and love our grand-children when they were small so that one day, when we were having a hard time, they would feel obligated to extend themselves. We simply loved them, and we were loved back in return.

My message to you is not to be afraid to lean on someone when you need the support. You may be surprised to find that there are other people who are as strong or stronger than you, and love has a way of finding solutions for the most complicated problems.

Sometimes I shake my head at the thought that I am being taken care of by the babies of the family. But then I remember that it is many years since they were babies and that I should not be surprised. I always saw great potential in my grandchildren, and now I have lived long enough to see that I was right.

We are not a traditional family unit, but we are a strong and happy one that has come out of the darkness into a bright time. Family can make your world immeasurably better, so I suggest you spend your life building a strong one, and then trust that together you can tackle every challenge in style.

CUTIE'S COUNSEL

1. Whatever is happening in children's lives, they should know that they can always come to their grandparents and get the straight dope. Honesty and unconditional love are the two things all grandparents should give to their grandchildren.

2. Be open to your relationship changing over the years. Children grow up, and adults grow old. Lean on the people who want to help you, especially if they used to lean on you.

3. Grandparents have seen it all. If you have a grandparent, be sure to ask a lot of questions. You'll be amazed at how much you'll learn about where you came from.

IF YOU'RE BORED, YOU'RE BORING

If you are as fortunate as I have been, one day you will wake up and realize that you're not young anymore, and you're not even middle-aged. But don't worry, you're not *old*—you've simply entered what I like to call the Bonus Years.

The Bonus Years were wonderful for Harry and for me. Our kids were out on their own and doing the things that kids do. We sold our business and were comfortable enough that we could afford to travel and treat ourselves, and to help our children when they asked.

The Bonus Years are the time when you get off the track that has dictated your activity for many years. You are no longer expected to please your parents and teachers, care for a baby, or serve your customers. Your time is your own, and from now on, your life will be what you make of it. If you want to be a bump on a log, you certainly may, but I think you will regret it. Whenever my grandchildren complain to me that they are bored, I tell them, "If you're bored, you're boring," and I guess that might be as close to a personal philosophy as I have. The idea of being bored is not part of my agenda. Life will not come find you and show you a good time; you have to go out and find it yourself.

Boredom is not a state I necessarily understand or recommend, especially not for young people. Children can be so silly. They think they already know all there is to know when they have experienced so little.

I would say, "Get some seeds and plant them and watch them grow, and then tell me you are bored." There is a saying that is very old and very true: "The world is so full of a number of things, I'm sure we should all be as happy as kings." Robert Louis Stevenson wrote that. My opinion is that any day when I am alive can be a joy. After breakfast, I look around and say to myself, "Isn't this great? I have all day to look at all the nice things around me." As long as your brain is working, you are in the pink.

Harry and I weren't looking to retirement as a chance to sit on our fannies and do nothing. We were excited about making this transition, because there was so much that we hadn't had the time, energy, or finances to do when we were younger.

I have to admit, after working for so many years, retirement took some getting used to. But we soon found a rhythm. We were not one of those couples who drives each other crazy when both of them are puttering around the house all day.

And we didn't really putter much. Harry was a busy bee. He golfed, fished, sailed, and played tennis, all things that he had enjoyed less frequently during our working years. He wasn't the athlete that he had been in his youth, but he always took pleasure in getting out into the sunshine and using his muscles.

As for me, I dedicated myself to all my favorite not-as-strenuous activities, volunteering for City of Hope, spending time with girlfriends, shopping for bargains, and spoiling my grandchildren. When I am feeling introspective, I recognize that most of my interests boil down to personal relationships. I love flowers and think they are beautiful, but I am too lazy to raise them. I could never be a musician, because practicing would be too isolating. But people are fascinating. I have always been interested in my reactions to others and their reactions to me. So while Harry played outside, I looked for people to connect with. My life has been very full in that regard. People always appreciate it when you show an interest in them.

Outside of our hobbies, Harry and I continued to spend a lot of time together. I think that is very important for retired couples; otherwise, they might forget who they are married to. If you don't already have things you like to do together, go out and find some. There is no excuse for not developing shared passions, since that is an essential ingredient in keeping any love affair alive. So get up off your duff and find these passions. You can play cards, take a walk, visit a museum, go out exploring, sit down to a meal, and have a conversation. The world is your oyster, and your partner is there to shuck, share, and enjoy it with you.

Also, I think it's very important to maintain a social circle. As much as you love your sweetheart, there should be other people to whom you confide and with whom you spend time. Don't make the mistake of being too busy to see your friends, or you might be surprised to discover you no longer have any. Having plans on the calendar helps you look forward to the days ahead.

In the mornings, for many years, we met our friends for a mid-morning breakfast gathering we called the Coffee Klatch. There were more than a dozen participants in our informal club, mostly married couples, but a few singles as the years went on. So even accounting for trips out of town, doctor's visits, and so on, on any given morning we could always count on seeing some of our friends without the need to plan the date. We found it a great way to start the day. And really, shouldn't every day after you've retired be a sort of party?

I know that some people are not fans of McDonald's restaurants and the fast food they serve, but we found our local branch to be the perfect location for this get-together. McDonald's was always very clean, the restaurant and the bathrooms, too. It had big tables scattered around the room, so we could break off into groups. The young people behind the counter were very friendly and accommodating. We liked McDonald's breakfast menu, but the servers didn't mind or notice if we brought our own matzo from home sometimes, and they always made sure to reserve our favorite tables.

Our loyalty was secured when McDonald's had a special promotion on what it called a "bottomless coffee mug." If you purchased this mug from the counter, McDonald's promised that anytime you brought it back, you could fill it up with coffee at no charge.

Well, you didn't have to tell me twice! Harry and I promptly purchased our magic mugs, and we started to get our money's worth out of them. After we finished our coffee, I would wrap the mugs up in napkins, place them in my purse, wash them at home, and bring them back to the Coffee Klatch next morning. Our friends all did the same.

Over the years, those mugs got stained and cracked. If you wanted to be fresh, you might say they were a lot like Harry and me. But like Harry and me, those mugs kept coming back to the Coffee Klatch most mornings, ready to socialize and hold more coffee. Some of our friends gave up coffee on doctor's orders; others lost or broke their mugs. But we held out until McDonald's got a new manager, who announced that he didn't know anything about some long-ago bottomless-coffee-mug promotion, and from now on, we'd have to buy our coffee like everybody else. But the joke was on him, because although we liked coffee just fine, we were equally happy to drink hot water with Sweet'N Low in it, and so we did.

When I was a girl, I had no idea that I would live into my nineties. Such longevity was not commonplace then. But I instinctively understood that being alive was a privilege and a pleasure, so I have always made the effort to stay engaged in the world around me. I did not want to be bored or boring, and with a few momentary exceptions, this philosophy has served me well.

So my advice to you is, don't wait to retire to start enjoying your existence. Keep your ears and eyes open. Have some savoir faire. There's a lot not to be bored about. Make every day the most fulfilling day it can be, and you will find that as you make many transitions throughout what I hope will be a long and healthy life, in each one there remains one constant: you like who you are and where you're standing and feel excited to see what will happen next.

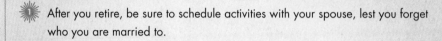

CUTIE'S COUNSEL

1. After you retire, be sure to schedule activities with your spouse, lest you forget who you are married to.

2. Maintain an active social circle to keep your spirits high. You don't have to go to McDonald's every morning like we did, but don't neglect the social whirl. Friendships outside the home keep you young.

3. Don't wait until after you retire to do the things you are dreaming about. None of us know how much time we've got, and this life is for enjoying.

MAKING MISTAKES

There's one tender subject that nobody really wants to talk about but everybody should: making mistakes. We all do it, although most of us would rather pretend that we have not. It is a funny frailty of human beings that all of us like to imagine that we are perfect, although we are certain that nobody else is.

A mistake can be big or it can be small, but I can assure you it is never more damaging than when the person who has made it tries to sweep the whole incident under a rug. You do not have to advertise your errors to the world, but you must not hide them from yourself. For example, in recent years I came to recognize that Harry had been putting my needs before his in many ways. Attentiveness can be a lovely quality in a husband, but when it meant that he was neglecting his own interests to focus on mine, that did not help either one of us to be a completely fulfilled person. As he aged and became less athletic, he spent more time around the house, and I think he was missing the private time that every man needs in his marriage. We were always very happy as a couple, but maybe he could have benefited from more individual time, or social activities away from me. I wish now I had recognized what was happening earlier and encouraged him to spend more time with his male friends or just off doing his own thing. I guess it is always easier to recognize your missteps in retrospect.

Whatever else mistakes are, they are best of all opportunities for learning. When you realize you have misjudged a situation or a person, or have acted rashly or carelessly, your first step should be to deal with the immediate fallout and to get back on track. Your second step should be to look at what has happened and try to understand why, so you can avoid repeating this mistake in the future.

Should you make a mistake and learn from it, it was not really a mistake. Should you make a mistake and let it happen again and again in different permutations, then you are not using your brains. Wake up! Everything that hurts or challenges you is a chance to live a better life tomorrow. I don't have much patience with people who treat unhappiness as a carousel ride or who decorate the rut they are in with curtains and Chinese vases.

Of course, when you are all wrapped up in your life and its problems, it can be difficult to distinguish actual mistakes from ordinary circumstances. Introspection is key. If you are feeling badly, try to understand what has made you feel that way. Maybe there is something you are doing repeatedly that you really ought to stop. Maybe there is more than one thing that's off-key, and together they are compounding the problem.

Even at my age, when I realize I have made a mistake, it is still a shock. You get into the habit of thinking you know what you are doing. I am most upset if I recognize that I've hurt another person by my carelessness. It's no big deal to take a wrong turn on the street or to use the wrong word in conversation. But an action that leaves another human being feeling worse than when you got there is something I always wish to avoid. I hope that I do not step on other people's toes. I don't wish to hurt other people, and I hope they will return the courtesy.

A Facebook friend asked me if I thought that it was possible to really forgive and forget. I told her that I do believe in forgiveness. But before you can forgive another person, you have got to be able to forgive yourself. Otherwise, you can't get out of bed in the morning. As for for-getting, I don't think anyone ever truly forgets a wrong. You remember, but, hopefully, you are able to accept and move on. I have always tried to learn from my mistakes and grow from them. That part never stops. Even at ninety-four, I feel like I am learning new things about myself and the world every day.

If in your mistake you have hurt another person, you should apologize and try to make that person whole again. Simply taking responsibility for your hurtful actions is a wonderful way to start feeling good about your-self again, and it's the rare person who will not accept a sincere apology and tell you to please forget about it.

If you have taken a turn in your life that is not working out, take a deep breath and figure out how you can get back to a better place—not right that minute, because that is usually not possible, but thoughtfully and patiently. Every little step in the right direction shifts your perspective, and a fresh perspective is the key to staying engaged with your life.

One way in which I judge the character of a person is by how grace-fully he or she handles an unexpected jolt. It's easy to look elegant when everything is going your way, but it's when things go amiss that you can see what a person is really made of. Practice keeping your cool when little stuff goes wrong, and you can work your way up to dealing with the big problems that may come along.

Some people are devastated by their mistakes. They sit around brood-ing over the past, wondering, "What if I had done it this way, or that way?" Don't give your mistakes that much power over you. You made a mistake; you have recognized it—now fix it, stop worrying, and move on. Nobody is perfect, and who would want to be? You can never change the past. I think that your mistakes can be what make you interesting, and if nothing else, they should keep you humble. So forgive yourself and start to live in the moment—which is a very lovely place and exactly where you belong.

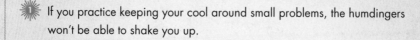

CUTIE'S COUNSEL

1. If you practice keeping your cool around small problems, the humdingers won't be able to shake you up.

2. Unless you are able to forgive yourself, you will never be able to forgive another. Don't expect perfection, but demand respect and honesty. If someone is truly sorry, forgive him or her and move on.

3. When you make a big mistake, don't pretend it never happened. Put it on the dining-room table and perform an autopsy. The bigger the boo-boo, the more you can learn and grow from it.

LATE-LIFE TRANSITIONS

Aging is an interesting experience, and like most transitions in this life, the quality of your experience will depend on your attitude. The first time somebody asks if you are entitled to "the senior discount," you might be tempted to deny it and slap the full price down on the counter. But with time you'll get used to being an old person and with having the outside world acknowledge it.

Once you're comfortable with the idea, there are a lot of benefits. Those discounts can be nice. People hold doors open for you and ask if they can carry your packages to the car. Even if you used to think you had to be superwoman or superman and do it all and more, as you age and slow down, you cut yourself some slack. You stop worrying so much about how your hair looks or if your figure is the right shape because you recognize that it's simply not possible to comb or diet your way to the physical ideal you see in magazines or on television. You get to be comfortable in your skin, and you feel more tolerant of other people. But at the same time, you no longer feel the need to hold your tongue when somebody is rude or annoying. Old folks don't have anything left to prove, so they get to simply enjoy being themselves.

When I was a young woman, I wondered if Harry would still find me attractive as I aged, and I worried that my feelings for him might change as he did. But we discovered that as our bodies grew fatter or skinnier, as we lost hair or grew it in peculiar places, our attraction for each other stayed intact. To the outside world, he may have been a roly-poly, bald-headed grandpa, but he never looked like one to me. No, he always looked like my sweetheart. If you had gone back in time to show the young me a photograph of the little old man who I still loved after seventy-three years, I am not sure that I would have recognized him, unless he was smiling, and then I might have asked, "Is that Harry's great-grandfather?" Year after year, he always looked familiar to me. I feel that he kept his looks through his whole life, which is to say he was very handsome as a boy, as a middle-aged man, and as an elderly gentleman. Plus, he had such a sweet disposition, and everyone knows that kind people are more beautiful. I never got tired of looking at him. When you have a mature love relationship, I guess that your attraction grows up along with the rest of you. It's like an old pair of shoes: not so perfect on the outside, but so very comfortable. You understand one another. It just fits.

Getting older sounds scarier than it is. If you live your life one day at a time, then you ease into the changes. If you have friends, if you have family, if you love yourself and do what you can to help others, then you can forget about aging and just focus on living. And then one day, maybe you will look in the mirror and discover—wow, you're ninety-four (I still can't believe it).

For Harry and me, one of the hardest things about aging was recognizing the need to change how we lived. You get set in your ways and think that you can go on the same way forever, even though little issues have a way of turning into medium-sized issues and worse.

Sometimes something bad has to happen before you can look up to see the writing on the wall. We used to drive a lot, thinking nothing of making the 150-mile round trip to visit our son and his family. When you are from Los Angeles, long drives are no big deal. Then one evening, driving home after seeing the kids, we had an accident.

Young people have accidents, too, of course, but as we recovered and talked together, we recognized that it was pretty draining to make a long drive, play with the children, eat a heavy meal, and drive home again. So we scaled back on the driving, and the kids came up to see us or we met on our side of the middle.

But we were *very* lucky. We ought to have cut back on our driving before we crashed our car. We could have killed ourselves or hurt somebody else.

So my advice to you is not to be as oblivious as we were. If something is too much for you, admit it. You do not always have to be the person who bends, and there is no shame in asking for help or consideration, especially if it makes your life easier and the world a safer place.

I wish that I could tell you that after the car accident, Harry and I changed our ways. But the fact is, there were other aspects of our life that were getting out of hand, but we really did wish to not see them. Our oldest grandchild, Kim, could see that we needed help around the house, but we didn't want to hear it. We insisted that everything was fine, end of story. Kim did not agree. We were not ready to relinquish our independence. So there were some arguments, and we were all frustrated. (This chapter is a good example of how *not* to behave.)

Eventually, we had another crisis. I had a heart attack, and while I was recovering, our daughter, Carol, died. Just a few months later, our son Jan died. Both deaths were unexpected. We were devastated. Harry wasn't in any shape to take care of me, but we still resisted getting a professional in to help us. We were anxious about the idea of living with a strange person, we didn't wish to spend the money, and, most of all, we were reluctant to admit that we could not live alone in our home.

We did the best that we could, but, frankly, it was not sufficient. I lost a lot of weight, and, through carelessness, I stopped taking my heart medication regularly. Harry fell a couple of times, and he couldn't get up on his own, nor could I lift him. Frequently, I would make a telephone call, then forget to hang up the phone, which meant a security guard from our gated community would have to come check on us when a worried family member couldn't get through. We found this quite embarrassing, and yet it kept on happening. I wonder if my subconscious was trying to send a message: "Help us, please!"

187

We were no longer the people we imagined ourselves to be, and we couldn't believe it, or did not wish to. It seemed easier to shut our eyes to the reality and pretend that everything was fine, end of story. But even as we kept saying everything was all right, our own voices sounded less assured. We knew we were in trouble, but after insisting for so many years that we could handle it, we did not know how to ask for help.

Eventually, our grandchildren made the decision for us, and they moved us into an assisted-living facility. Although we had not liked the idea, the reality was surprisingly pleasant. We took our favorite things to our nice apartment, which felt like being young marrieds again. One of the things that sold us was the gorgeous view of one of the historic bridges over the Los Angeles River, and another was our two walk-in closets, one for my *chazerai* (that's Jewish for "clutter") and one for Harry's. Even though we no longer had a house to look after, he brought a small tool kit with him, and often I would find him standing in his closet, holding one of his tools in his hands. After so many years as a tinkerer, I guess this was just a feeling that he enjoyed.

Well, what a change! We had shed all of our big responsibilities, and that meant we could simply enjoy one another. We did not have to go grocery shopping or plan our meals. Instead, someone would knock on our door and remind us that it was dinnertime, and we'd go down to a pretty dining room, sit with nice people, and enjoy healthy fare. We didn't have to remember if we had swallowed our pills yet, because there were nurses to dispense them, take our blood pressure, and look after us if we caught cold. And ultimately, what more do you need than a roof over your head, good food, and pleasant people around you? With all that, we were content.

But the best part was the change in our relationships with our granddaughters. Now that we were living closer to them, we could see much more of each other. Instead of being worried sick, with their visits packed with running errands and dealing with whatever crisis had hit our home since the last time, they could relax and have fun with us, and we with them. We used our extra time together to start The OGs blog, which has resulted in the book you are reading.

If you had asked us earlier, we would have told you that we were not interested in leaving our house, yet the move to an apartment in an assisted-living facility was a good one, and one we should probably have made years earlier. Well, you know what they say about hindsight.

We thought we had our plan for aging all sewn up. When we were young retirees, we purchased a home in a seniors-only community in Ventura County called Leisure Village. We loved it. There was a big swimming pool where I could do water aerobics, a golf course and tennis courts for Harry, a library, theatrical programs, even a television studio. We made a lot of friends, and we never lacked for company at the card table or over dinner.

But although Leisure Village was a wonderful community for active seniors, it really had nothing to offer us as we transitioned into what is known in the geriatric community as super seniors. This doesn't mean that we were comic-book characters but that we were getting to be extremely old. The living arrangements that had been satisfactory for us when we were independent became more challenging with time. It was hard to keep the house clean or eat a proper meal three times a day. Harry had stopped driving, and I was unwell, so if we wanted to go shopping or to a doctor's appointment, we had to call a senior transport van, then wait on the hot sidewalk for the driver to come back again. It was a pain in the neck, and sometimes it seemed easier to just skip the trip.

The funny thing about ignoring problems is that the effects are cumulative. If you have given up driving and don't care to pay for cab service, you are not likely to go shopping for food as often as you should. If you don't eat enough, you get too skinny. If you're too skinny and you bang your knee, it bruises something fierce. If your knee really hurts, you might not bother to keep up on your daily exercise or social activities, so instead you sit on your duff and watch TV. Before you know it, you're depressed,

189

weak, and lonesome, and you have completely forgotten that the original problem was that you had given up driving and didn't care to pay for cab service.

Moving out of our house eliminated a great many small problems and permitted us to enjoy our life together in a way in which we had not been able to do for quite some time. It put a new spring in our steps, and I would recommend that other people who are getting along in years not wait as long as we did to make the change. Leisure Village had been a great place to spend our late middle age, but we outgrew it. And because we did not make our own plans, it was left to our grandchildren to take on the responsibility that should have been ours.

If I could go back and talk with my slightly younger self, I would say that we ought to have a plan for what to do if we lived to be quite old. I would sit down with my husband and decide what was best for us, then talk with our family to make sure we were all on the same page. Also, I would tell myself to accept more assistance. There is no shame in asking for some help, and it does not mean you lose all your independence when you do so. In fact, by actively accepting the help that you need, you are remaining in control, which feels wonderful.

But we didn't expect to receive so many years on this earth, and before we realized it, our age crept up on us. Harry's parents were both gone before he married me. My mother lived to be eighty, and my father died when he was seventy-six. My mother left her big house and moved into an apartment, but only after my father was gone. So as long as Harry and I had each other, we simply expected that we'd stay in our home and everything would be great.

Without really articulating it, we just assumed that we, too, would pass away at around the age of eighty. *Well, when we moved out of our house, Harry was ninety-six and I was ninety-one!*

It just goes to show that you cannot predict what is in store for you, and just because you are older, you cannot stop planning for your future. Modern medicine is amazing, and you might live to be one hundred or even older. So do yourself a favor and make a plan for the possibility that you will become a super senior, too. Should you do so, I hope you will take some of my advice and be a very happy, tuned-in old person. You deserve it!

CUTIE'S COUNSEL

Rare are those individuals who can take care of themselves every day of their lives. Accept that you will be sick sometimes, and while you are healthy, figure out who you can turn to should you ever need assistance.

Make a plan for your future, and share it with your family. If you just bump along aimlessly through life, you are bound to fall in a hole eventually.

If something is more than you can handle, admit it. You aren't doing yourself any favors by pretending everything is fine when you are actually struggling.

LOSING HARRY

When you are twenty years old and marry an older man of twenty-five, you think nothing of the age difference. Sure, he is somewhat more mature, more experienced in the ways the world works, but you are essentially peers. When Harry was forty, I was thirty-five. When he was eighty, I was seventy-five. He went through each big birthday ahead of me, but we felt that we were walking hand in hand.

There were times when I was sick, or he was sick, but we both had strong constitutions and always bounced back from our various health crises. That was how it had always been and what we were used to.

Things started to change a year after we moved into our assisted-living facility. Harry got up to do something, tripped, and cracked his femur. His surgeon told us that he must have an operation or he would not be able to walk again. If he didn't get the operation, he'd spend most of his life in a chair or flat on his back, and there was a very real danger that he would contract pneumonia from being inactive and that this would not be something he could recover from.

So there was really only one reasonable choice, and Harry got the operation. He came through it in good shape, but when it was time to do his physical therapy and start walking again, he struggled. His eyesight and hearing were both fading, and I don't think anyone had realized how much he had been compensating for these missing sensations before his accident. But now, unable to see or hear clearly, and needing a walker or cane to support his weakened legs, he was skittish about walking into the unknown.

Where he had always been a fighter who worked hard to bounce back from illness, now he began to ask why he couldn't just sit in his chair and listen to music or take a nap. What was so urgent that he needed to get up and walk? If he didn't feel like walking, wasn't that answer enough?

Day after day, I sat by his bed in the nursing ward, where he had been moved to recover. I took my meals with Harry, and I sat with him in the sunshine, holding hands and watching the flowers blow in the wind. I crawled into bed with him and napped. I waited while his therapist and grandchildren took him for his walks, which he got regardless of his questions about why he could not nap instead.

In the evening, someone would remind me to go back to my apartment across the courtyard, and I would go there to sleep and have breakfast with my friends, but then I would return to Harry's side. We didn't talk much. I didn't do much. It seemed easier to doze in his bed rather than to go outside and soak up the sunshine. Harry was slowing down, and I was slowing down with him.

I wanted to move into his hospital room permanently, but the girls discouraged me. They reminded me that we had a nice apartment, and there was no guarantee that it would still be available when we were ready to leave the nursing ward. They reminded me that I was not ill and that I could spend as much time with Harry as I wished as long as I passed the night in my own room. I realize now that they were concerned that if I moved into Harry's room, and he died, I would not have a life of my own to go back to. They were right.

So I sat by his side and I thought a lot. And one day, I told the girls that I missed my husband and that I felt like *he had gotten old on me.* I felt guilty for even saying this out loud, but once I did, I found that it was easier to deal with my conflicted feelings. I began to spend more time in my room. I played some bingo, and I won more than once. I went shopping for new shoes, reviewed some restaurants, and made videos for our blog. I got a strawberry blonde rinse in my hair. I stopped sleeping so much.

I still visited Harry every day, but instead of just parking my carcass in his room and waiting for dinnertime, I spent some quality time with my husband before getting back to the day's activities. If he wanted to talk, we talked. If he wanted a smooch, we kissed. If he was feeling bushed, as he often was, we spoke for a few moments and I left him to his napping. Mostly, we sat side by side on a couch in the hallway, holding hands and listening to the caged birds singing to us. Sometimes Harry would whistle to them, too.

And so this is how, after seventy-three years in which we were inseparable, Harry and I slipped apart. My older man of a husband had become, at long last, an old man. But I was not an old woman yet. I wasn't ready to lie down and miss out on all the adventures that life still had in store for me.

I was very fortunate, because it did not fall on me to be my husband's caregiver. At this stage of my life, it would have been too much for me to handle, and not good for him, either. Between the nursing staff at our assisted-living facility and our grandchildren and me, Harry got the attention that he needed.

I have learned a lot about what it means to care for another person who cannot look after him- or herself, and I worry about the caregivers. As I told a Facebook friend—an overwhelmed caregiver seeking advice because he volunteered to help a friend's sick and cranky mother—it is a very difficult job, especially when you are looking after an adult who is used to being independent. You cannot control how the sick person feels or behaves, but you can be mindful of the stress you're under. There is no shame in admitting when you can't continue, reaching out for help, or taking a time-out to look after yourself. It does not make you a bad person if you recognize that you have reached your limit in looking after another person. I think the caregivers of the world are diamonds, and they deserve much more respect and support than they receive.

But back to my husband. After his surgery, Harry lost his appetite. He'd eat, but not with the gusto he once had. They say your stomach shrinks if you don't eat enough, and then you don't want to eat, which is a vicious cycle.

Harry lost some weight, and his doctor was concerned that without strong muscles, it would continue to be a struggle for him to get out of his chair and walk. He was pretty weak and becoming disinterested in things around him. So the decision was made to fatten him up with liquid nourishment through a tube and see if that helped.

During this process, he went to the hospital for a few nights, where he was checked out from stem to stern. This is where his doctor discovered that Harry's heart was beating on borrowed time. With Harry's history of heart troubles that spanned almost forty years, the muscles and arteries were reaching the limit of what they could do for him. My sweetheart's big, strong heart was wearing out.

The thing about having a body is that it's a machine, and like all machines, eventually wear and tear is going to catch up with you. You can delay the inevitable by taking good care of yourself, eating well, staying active, looking both ways when crossing streets, seeing your doctor regularly, and all of those dull tasks, but if you live long enough, your body is going to fall apart. You might need a new knee. You might have to say good-bye to a breast. Maybe you'll just lose a few teeth and your hair. But aging means changing, and in the end, most people age their way right off this planet. That was what was happening to Harry, and although I was sad to see it, and frightened at the thought of being without him, I was also lucky, because it was not sudden and I had the opportunity to live with the idea while still having my husband close to me.

On the day he died, I visited him in the hospital. He had been put in a special private room that had been decorated like the cell in which a Korean Buddhist monk would live. It was very beautiful, with bamboo panels and a colorful backlit photographic mural of a river and trees in his line of sight. He was there because he was very old, and the hospital staff considered him venerable and deserving of special respect. When I came to visit, they treated me with great kindness, too. Chinta told the nurse on duty how long we had been married, and I could hear the phrase whispered as I walked down the hall: "Seventy-three years together!" We sat together and held hands. I kissed him and told him he would be home soon. He said my name and told me that he loved me. It was a good visit. Every visit was good.

As I left, it did not occur to me that we would not see each other again. I thought the doctors would finish their tests and send him home, and he'd keep on going for a while longer. But around midnight, he spoke with one of the nurses who was checking on him, and when she asked how he was feeling, he told her that he felt good and that she was a good nurse. She continued on her rounds, stopped in to see him about fifteen minutes later, and found that he had died. When I was taken to him maybe an hour later, his wrinkled old face was peaceful and still beautiful to me. I cried and held his cooling hands, and when I was ready, my grandchildren took me home to sleep in my own bed.

We buried Harry in the lawn plot that we had selected together, not far from where my parents are interred. He loved the tropics, so we dressed him in his favorite green Hawaiian shirt, with his Masonic ring on his finger. He looked handsome, and just like himself.

We asked a friend to read from *The Bhagavad Gita,* the two-thousand-year-old Hindu scripture that he had enjoyed discussing with Chinta, a philosophy student, during the last years of his life. The passage selected concerned the consoling notion that nothing that has been alive can ever truly cease to exist:

As a man throweth away old garments and putteth on new, even so the dweller in the body, having quitted its old mortal frames, entereth into others which are new. The weapon divideth it not, the fire burneth it not, the water

corrupteth it not, the wind drieth it not away; for it is indivisible, incon-
sumable, incorruptible, and is not to be dried away: it is eternal, universal,
permanent, immovable; it is invisible, inconceivable, and unalterable; there-
fore, knowing it to be thus, thou shouldst not grieve.

The graveside service ended, and we sat quietly in the shade, tears sliding down our faces, holding each other's hands, exhausted and in pain. Soon we would have to get up, get back into our cars, and leave the cemetery. But for now, we were in the quiet moment between the ceremony and the return to real life. I felt like I ought to say something, and I looked into my brain to see if there was something profound there.

As I sat there on a folding chair next to the hole in which my husband's body had been placed, all I could think of was something ridiculous— true, yet ridiculous. I paused for a moment, unsure if I should say my thought aloud. And then I thought, "What the hell?" And I turned to my granddaughters and said, "What a waste! To bury that man with a full set of teeth!" They stared at me, shocked, for a moment, and then the laughter began, hysterical, but such a relief. Harry *did* have gorgeous teeth. And I was going to miss him like hell, but I was going to live.

CUTIE'S COUNSEL

1. Understand that you must age at your own pace, not your partner's pace. You are an individual, and it is possible that your paths may not be the same length.

2. Allow yourself to feel upset about the changes that aging brings to you and to your partner, and don't be afraid to talk about these feelings. Hiding from them encourages you to let your life slip out of your control.

3. In some marriages, one partner has the big mouth and the other stays more in the background. But if the big mouth is ever sick, the quieter partner will need to stand up and be his or her advocate. Have a plan for a crisis, and make sure your partner knows your wishes.

A SOLO ACT

And so this is how, after seventy-three years as the wife of Harry Cooper, I found myself a single gal at the age of ninety-three. It's an idea that took some getting used to, but I've decided to stick with it. After all, Harry was always five years my senior, which means that he had five years to sow his wildest oats before I came along and made him be good. Maybe this means that the next five years are all for me to enjoy, so that we come out equal in the end.

It's not as if I can afford to sit in the corner and mope. There are a lot of people who need me. I was a little skeptical about giving advice on the Internet when my grandchildren suggested it, but I have to admit that they know me pretty well. When people tell me their problems, it is almost instinct for me to blurt out what I see as the clear solution. I can't explain it, but I am just full of answers. So, you will often find me at the computer, reading messages from mothers and fathers and daughters and sons, and trying to give them a little dose of my wisdom to help them get through another day.

My grandkids tell me I am a celebrity, but I don't really feel any differently. It's not like I swam the English Channel or climbed Mount Everest. Fame is not anything that has affected me. I don't put more cream in my coffee or use a different fork with dinner. However, both Harry and I liked the idea that we were being acknowledged for having a happy marriage, even though we felt like this was no big deal. But isn't it a sweet thing to be known for? And I must admit that there is something to this celebrity business, because we were recognized a couple of times at restaurants. This was a nice experience, because when the waitress was the one doing the recognizing, it meant extra fudge on our sundaes.

Before I began giving advice, I was a fan of the genre. I always read Dear Abby and Ann Landers, and I watched the judges on TV. Ninety percent of the time I have agreed with the advice I heard. Most advice is pretty good; the trouble comes because not everyone who asks is ready to take it. Sometimes, people come back to me with the same questions, as if my advice would change with the wind.

This is not a job for the faint of heart. A person might take my advice and get into deep water, so it is important not to be flippant, even if the problem seems ridiculous or if the person annoys me in some way. You must have your hat on properly and your feet grounded. You must be impartial and recognize that you are only hearing one side of most problems. An advice lady is like a rabbi or a doctor—my fans take me seriously. I respect them, and I think that shows.

Some people have problems that I find familiar. Maybe they are feeling overworked and having trouble getting to the things that matter in their marriage. Some people are struggling with issues that are new to me, but I hope that my advice is universal enough to help them get on firmer footing and feel more in control of their lives.

There have been times when I've sought advice, too. When asking for advice, you need to take it for what it's worth. Weigh the suggestions, your opinion of the person giving them, and the relevance of the advice to your life. It is fine to say "thank you very much" and to use only a portion, or none, of the advice you receive. If it doesn't make sense, discard it. But I do think that if someone takes the time to suggest a course of action, you should at least pretend to appreciate it.

Also, there is no shame in changing your direction. If you have done something and it doesn't work out, undo it and try something else. As long as you're alive, you are entitled to change your mind and change your life. People who understand that will always be happier than people who do not.

So if you take my advice and it helps, bully for you. If it doesn't, try something else. If you made a wrong move, the world doesn't have to come to an end. I hope you end up on the right path for you. If you keep your eyes open and respect yourself, I am sure that you will.

I am an older gal now, and I don't have the oomph that once powered my existence and made me known as the lady who would never sit down at her own dinner parties. I no longer throw dinner parties, and I am content to remain in my chair at the soirées that I attend. The new me is happy to take things pretty slowly, enjoying favorite foods and my power naps, with occasional excursions to see the sunshine and the flowers and whatever adventure the children have planned for me today. I like bingo when I win, exploring Los Angeles, and listening to classic tunes from the 1940s and 1950s.

If you can count your blessings, that's a good activity. I'd much rather focus on the sweet than the sour stuff. If it's a beautiful day and the breeze is ruffling my hair, that's a great feeling. I can walk down the street without limping, and that's marvelous. I look into the mirror and ask, "Is that old lady really me?" Then I reply, "Barbara Cooper, that's you, and you are almost 100 years old. You are in good health. Your family that you have left, you love. Your family that are gone are in God's hands. You'd better be happy with what you've got!" Well, I have no complaints. Thank you, God.

At this stage of my life, I feel more like a receiver than a broadcaster. I am here and pleased to observe the world as it goes by and to contribute my insights if they are requested. I'm not looking for busywork to keep me out of trouble. Being old has a certain Zen-like quality. It's easier to be patient, and I've lost that old feeling that if I am awake, there is always something I should be doing. It helps that I have downsized and don't have a house to look after any more.

You don't notice it because it happens so slowly, but every person slows down. You adjust your life to the energies and responsibilities that you have. You are who you have become, and there is no shame in adjusting.

I think about Harry every day. When I am dozing, it sometimes seems as if he is still here, and I might get up to tell him something and only realize then that he is no longer available to me. I do not like living without him, but I recognize that the alternative is not for me. If Harry was here, I know that he would tell me, "You cannot fight City Hall, Barbara. Face facts. We had a good life together; we loved each other. And from now on, you must do the best with what is left. Pick up your pieces and live." That is what Harry tells me in my dreams, and it is what I intend to do.

Some days are easier than others. I am grieving. They say that grief comes in stages, but it is not as simple as that. It will proceed exactly as it does and when it does. I try not to judge myself for how I am feeling, to be where I am and be kind to myself. I try to treat myself like Harry would treat me. And I know that it is going to get better.

I do not think of myself as a widow. It seems to me that Harry is someplace around. I kind of forget that he has died. He did not consult with me first, so as far as I am concerned, this is nothing that has been sanctioned.

I don't complain to God, because I know that if I did, God would tell me that I am not the only one who has lost a husband. And after seventy-three happy years, who am I to raise a stink? If it hurts, I just have to learn to be stronger. This is my life, and I accept it. I am lucky to have had all the happiness I've known, and I can still feel happy. It is wonderful to be alive, and as long as I am here, there is somebody who remembers everything about Harry Cooper. Isn't that something worth living for?

I think the secret to going on after a loss is simply to focus on how amazing it is to be alive. There is something to give you joy in every moment. It is all in your perspective. By feeling happy, you are not being selfish or showing disrespect for the person you have lost. If you had a good relationship, then you can be realistic when it ends. All things do. Smiling does not take the sadness away, just like the sadness does not make it impossible to smile again.

Maybe the key is simply optimism. When I look at myself, I see a lucky lady, even though I have lost my husband and my children. I am an average person who can count my blessings, acknowledge my losses, and recognize that there are some things that I cannot control. My choice is to go on, to live, and to be content with what I have got. It is a very positive seat that I am sitting in. I would not ask for things to be different, because it is not in my power to know if that would be better or worse than what I have today. I am not prepared to take that gamble.

Some people get stuck in place and let the world slip away from them. They cease to be relevant. I am fortunate because even when I wanted to withdraw, I did not get the opportunity. There have always been those in my life who have encouraged me to step out into the light and shine, to talk it out when I was feeling blue, to recognize that I still matter.

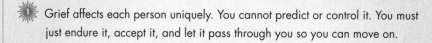

CUTIE'S COUNSEL

1. Grief affects each person uniquely. You cannot predict or control it. You must just endure it, accept it, and let it pass through you so you can move on.

2. Everyone who lives long enough to love deeply will experience great losses. Don't let fear of loss, or the losses themselves, take away your ability to enjoy the wonderful life that is yours.

3. Advice is good to give and good to receive, but when you get advice, your only obligation is a gracious "thank you." Feel free to toss out the bad advice that you get, just like you wouldn't eat a spoiled egg if someone gave it to you as a gift.

4. People are like plants, requiring care and nourishment to flourish. Be the loving gardener for every soul that you care about, and you will see each one of them transformed in ways you cannot imagine.

MY GREAT STROKE OF FORTUNE was that Harry Cooper fell in love with me. When he looked at this ordinary girl, he saw that she was beautiful, and funny, and intelligent, and kind. He had such high expectations for me that I felt I had to live up to them so as not to disappoint my Harry. Maybe I was not quite as wonderful as he thought I was, but I certainly tried to be, for him.

Together we made a family, Harry and me and our children growing up under the same roof, doing the best we could to love and understand one another. The years were long, and full of joy and challenges, but almost before we knew it, our kids were grown. And as we sent our son and daughter out into the world to make their own homes and relationships, Harry and I were back where we'd started, just the two of us, happy to find we were still so much in love.

And then I was blessed with sweet grandchildren, who looked at their little old grandma and saw someone who still had a lot to offer to the world. They tell me that my advice has a real impact, as do the kind people who thank me for helping them to make big decisions that have changed their lives.

This faith and love have changed my life and continue to shape it in incredible ways. If you want to see something beautiful happen, I suggest that you try to show the people you love how amazing you think they are, and then sit back and watch all the ways in which they will prove you right.

If there is a lesson to be learned from the silly story of *Barbara Cooper, world's oldest Internet advice lady,* it is this: never count yourself out. Every person has something to give, some love or some wisdom or a shoulder to cry upon. As long as you care about others, you have a reason to be on this earth. So go take your place in the grand scheme, and live your life with all your heart.

My wish for you, dear reader, is that you get the chance to enjoy and express yourself as I have done. I hope that you have or will find a love that you can grow up and grow old with and that you can look in the mirror and smile at who you see. If my ideas help you get there, then please remember little old Barbara and Harry Cooper sometimes, and pass along any wisdom that you find useful.

As for myself, if I can leave a little more love in the world than there was when I got here, then I think I've got something to feel good about and a reason to get out of bed tomorrow and continue being me.

ACKNOWLEDGMENTS

SOME BOOKS ARE SOLITARY CREATIONS, but this one took shape under the kind attention of so many lovely people that it cannot end without our giving thanks.

We are grateful to our supportive family, to our grandparents' caregivers and physicians, and to The OGs' sweet fans, whose enthusiasm inspired us to keep blogging and to look deeper to articulate the wisdom at the core of our grandparents' incredible relationship.

Thanks to our agent, Monika Verma, for asking if there was a book somewhere inside the blog and helping us to find it, and to our editor, Kate Woodrow, for her deft and sensitive understanding of the material.

Thank you to Doug Schreiber and Bob Weinberg for thoughtful counsel and warm friendship.

We appreciate the journalists who helped tell our grandparents' story, made them feel special, and introduced their blog to new visitors. Thank you, Michael Austin and Lee Cowan (*TODAY*), Rosemary Brennan (*Glamour*), Stephanie Chen and Josh Levs (CNN), Ari Seth Cohen (Advanced Style), Trish Crawford (*Toronto Star*), Matthew Fleischer (Fishbowl LA), Christal Gardiola (Shalom Life), Gloria Hillard (*All Things Considered*), Dikla Kadosh (*Jewish Journal*), Kate Linthicum (*Los Angeles Times*), Dave Malkoff (KTLA), Makael Mclendon and Kevin Simmons (*The Skorpion Show*), Steve Slon (The Connected Caregiver), Yoshikatsu Toyoda (*Tokudane Toukou Doga*), and Leslie Minora (*Village Voice*).

And finally, thank you to Richard Schave, who accepted our grandparents as if they were his own, and whose love and support shine through every page of this book.

—KIM COOPER AND CHINTA COOPER, LOS ANGELES